Social Entrepreneurship

Social Entrepreneurship

From Issue to Viable Plan

Terri D. Barreiro and Melissa M. Stone

First published in 2013 by
Business Expert Press, LLC
222 East 46th Street, New York, NY 10017
www.businessexpertpress.com

ISBN-13: 978-1-60649-516-2 (paperback)
ISBN-13: 978-1-60649-517-9 (e-book)

Business Expert Press Entrepreneurship and Small Business
Management collection

Collection ISSN: 1946-5653 (print)
Collection ISSN: 1946-5661 (electronic)

Cover and interior design by Exeter Premedia Services Private Ltd.,
Chennai, India

First edition: 2013

10 9 8 7 6 5 4 3 2 1

Printed in the United States of America.

Abstract

This book provides a guided deep dive into the early stages of venture development of social entrepreneurship. It introduces concepts that provide important insights necessary for social venture success. It introduces a set of entrepreneurial tools designed for the unique set of challenges faced in selecting and designing social entrepreneurial ventures. With this book as a guide, the reader can develop a feasible venture concept and communicate it effectively.

A passion to address social and environmental issues is the motivation for a growing number of entrepreneurs. Yet, effective approaches addressing these societal issues can be difficult to discern. Approaches cannot be well formulated using the traditional market place framework of traditional entrepreneurship. For example, traditional market and target market analyses miss important aspects of potential customer behavior. Cultural traditions, family structures, and community norms significantly influence human behavior. Without the knowledge about a specific community the missing perspective is too often discovered too late in the process. Undiscovered competitors, cultural practices that block adoption, and homemade alternatives can result in the demise of a start-up.

This book introduces concepts that frame new ways to approach information gathering and analysis for social entrepreneurial ideas. The book provides the reader guidance on:

- how to move from heart-tugging issues to social entrepreneurial opportunities with high potential;
- how to understand and assess the societal and policy environment in which the opportunity would be implemented;
- how to analyze and select the best approaches for that circumstance;
- how to frame a results focused approach; and
- how to communicate the product or new approach to gain investors, grants and community engagement.

Experienced nonprofit sector leaders have developed the concepts, principles, and application tools introduced here. A number of tools were developed by the authors and have been tested in communities across North America. Other tools introduced are modifications of standard business analysis tools that enable easier application in the social entrepreneurial environment. All the tools have been used in graduate courses and community settings.

The intended audience for this book includes people with a passion to make the world a better place, college students and business students seeking new ways to address unmet needs, students and others studying entrepreneurship and innovation (undergraduate and graduate students), executive education programs and training programs reaching the nonprofit sector managers and leaders, and public, nonprofit, and private sector intermediary organizations focused on addressing local region or national social or environmental issues.

Keywords

social entrepreneurship, feasibility analysis, entrepreneur, social entrepreneur, theory of change, logic model, public policy analysis, nonprofit.

Contents

CHAPTER 1

Introduction

All progress is precarious, and the solution of one problem brings us face to face with another problem.

Martin Luther King, Jr.

> ➢ *Hunger in America reports 49 million people in the United States were at risk for being hungry in 2010–1 in 6 people.[1] Why do people go hungry in the richest country in the world?*
>   - *Let's create a nation where everyone has enough to eat every day!*
> ➢ *Homeless in Minnesota, a triennial statewide study completed by Wilder Research of the Wilder Foundation, states, "On October 25, 2012, 10,214 homeless adults, youth and children—a 6 percent increase over the 2009 study."[2] Why are people homeless when there are so many empty buildings and houses in so many cities?*
>   - *Let's end homelessness in 10 years.*
> ➢ *Nearly one billion people lack a course of clean safe water in the world.[3] Why can't there be drinkable water everywhere in the world?*
>   - *Let's get potable water to all.*
> ➢ *Polio remains epidemic in 3 countries.[4] Why are people still getting polio?*
>   - *Let's stop Polio!*

An issue can be stated simply; so can a solution. But getting from a concern about the issue to an implementable solution is daunting. Entrepreneurial enthusiasm, generous philanthropy, and great amounts of human resources are not enough to address today's pressing issues.

Social entrepreneurs are taking on these issues and many more, striving to find better solutions. Social entrepreneurs create innovative solutions to immediate social problems and mobilize the ideas, capacities, resources, and social arrangements required for sustainable social transformations.[5]

But some solutions are more effective, create deeper change, and are more long-lasting than others. These solutions tend to take into account a clear understanding of the people experiencing the issues, the community, the social ecosystems, and the policy environment that are often at the heart of these issues. This more holistic perspective on the context surrounding issues allows the social entrepreneur to determine the real feasibility of an approach and avoid a premature or ill-advised launch.

All of us grow up and live in multiple social ecosystems and experience life's challenges from our own vantage point. Those experiences create frames of references, filters, and blinders that limit and sometimes block the collection and focus of important data. These filtering lenses come into play when searching to understand a problem. The first question we ask consciously or unconsciously when observing a new dilemma is "what am I observing?" We try to find a reference in our lives that gives us an analogy that explains what we are seeing. Our brains are pattern-making machines. We use our own education, culture, and experience to create frameworks for those patterns. These observations can lead to operating assumptions and strategies that may reflect more the lenses of the social entrepreneur than the actual experience of the people who are the target of the intervention. These assumptions are created without a more complete understanding of the complexities of the problems or issues. The social entrepreneur can be much more effective by recognizing his or her own perspectives and seeking out critical information on target populations, communities, and policy environments. Together this knowledge can improve the impact of a social venture plan on significant societal problems.

The purpose of this book is to provide the social entrepreneur, whether a novice or an experienced leader, with an understanding of the process needed to form a sustainable venture that has the goal of creating positive societal change. Our emphasis is on helping the social entrepreneur develop a sound understanding of how community, policy, and competitive environments affect the issue to be addressed, as well as a deeper understanding of those expected to be beneficiaries. A social entrepreneur's thinking may begin with a passion for a social issue, enthusiasm for a specific innovative solution or idea, or seeing a particular opportunity. What this book addresses is the frequent gap between these passions and enthusiasms and a venture's launch. Through building a deeper understanding of the beneficiaries and of the community, policy, and competitive environments of the issue, the social entrepreneur will have a realistic assessment of a venture's feasibility and, likely, a more potent venture project.

This book provides tools that help social entrepreneurs search and analyze a lot of information, allowing them to focus their energy and resources on solving important problems, changing services, products and systems, and doing so more successfully. And it guides the social entrepreneur to combine that new knowledge with a cohesive and feasible venture design.

The Feasibility Analysis for a Social Entrepreneurial Approach Is Different

A great deal of attention has been paid to feasibility assessments for market-place entrepreneurial ventures. In general, these approaches ask the entrepreneur to focus on collecting and assessing key information, including:

1. A market analysis: Analyzes the market place for the product or service including a review of the target market and the competition and an estimate of the size of the likely sales.

2. Product test results: What is the product or service and how does the target market respond it to? Market-focused entrepreneurial ventures tend to have a specific product or service that can be tested in real time—prototypes, beta versions, taste tests, and more give the entrepreneur observable reactions to the product and how it meets the customers' wants and needs.

3. An implementation plan: Describes what is needed to produce the product or service: the costs, the equipment and expertise needed, and the timeframe for production and may include a determination of the key leadership positions and expertise needed. An implementation plan often also includes a risk assessment and response plan including facing the market entry barriers, reviewing the suppliers needed, and the intellectual property dynamics.

4. A financial plan: A detailed picture of the financial projections and basics of the financial model including sources of funding, time frames for obtaining investors, and sales projections and more.

Far less attention, however, has been paid to the different, unique, and critical areas of feasibility assessment for social entrepreneurial ventures. Simply applying concepts from the for-profit world, like the aforementioned four types of analyses, does not work well for social entrepreneurial ventures. For example, social entrepreneurs often cannot complete a product or service test in a traditional way due to the vulnerability of those to be reached, the new nature of the product, the location of the potential clients, or the limited capacity of short-term measures of the expected impact. This book lays out different social entrepreneurial-based analyses that are key to the design of effective ventures.

The most important reason a new approach to feasibility assessment is needed, however, is because social entrepreneurial approaches often requires important service design, policy, public attitude, or service industry change goals. If a social entrepreneur is to effectively address this kind of broad systems change, then, as Bloom and Dees state, social entrepreneurs "must understand and often alter the social systems that create and sustain the problems in the first place."[6] Social entrepreneurs, more than their for-profit counterparts, must analyze the community, service infrastructure, and policy systems in which their ventures are embedded. It is those environments that formally or informally affect the focal issue. These systems are often complex, containing formal as well as informal entities with a stake in the issue the social entrepreneur is targeting. Government regulations, legal mandates, funding flows as well as formal and informal networks and community institutions often present both constraints *and* additional opportunities for innovation and change. In addition attention must be paid to potential partners, competitors, and the forces that encourage or discourage entry into the system.

The Social Venture Environment

Social entrepreneurs often work in contested spaces because many of their ventures address public problems that are the consequence of longstanding and complex social and/or economic inequities. These issues have multiple, often conflicting constituencies who have a stake in how the problem is defined and solutions are framed.[7] Their new ideas challenge these existing powerful institutional interests and the status quo.

To confound the social entrepreneur, the issue often exists in dynamic policy environments that are likely to impact the feasibility of any given venture. For example, public bureaucracies or government-contracted nonprofit organizations may already be involved in implementing similar programs as part of specific local, state, or federal policy goals. Or, regulations may exist that could substantially constrain the venture and threaten its feasibility. Sometimes these environments have clear and distinct boundaries, but most often they have overlapping, interconnected, and interdependent kinds of dynamics that can appear to be at odds with one another. In other words, many ventures inadvertently walk right into the world of politics and policy making. Without early attention to understanding this environment, the social entrepreneur may encounter barriers that block actions.

Cultural variations in how an issue impacts a population can change dramatically from community to community within a region, a state, across states, and across countries. Tim Reardon, Minneapolis-based consultant and initiative leader for social issue collaborations told Terri Barreiro in an interview in March 2013 about his own recognition of impact variations and the resulting unexpected barriers to issue progress. His example was about the Somali population in Minnesota, the largest population of Somalis outside of Africa. This population of new immigrants comes from a rich tribal decision-making structure that honors the formal and informal community leaders that have influence and are called upon to make decisions on behalf of their community. On many occasions, this Somali community within Minnesota has found its traditional ways of resolving conflict and making decisions challenged by the legal, political, and cultural norms of the United States. A high-profile case of domestic violence within the community was being prosecuted by the state court system and encountered the wrath of Somali leaders who wanted to apply their community problem-solving methods to resolve the situation. The US legal system prevailed, but at a cost of alienating many members of the Somali community and creating conflict among the members, some of whom wanted to assimilate to the American way of doing business, and others who wanted to preserve their unique cultural norms of problem solving and honoring their elders and religious traditions. Efforts to intervene in the Somali culture that are unaware of the unique nature of this population are likely to be "dead on arrival" when they encounter the strength of this cultural group and its strong interpersonal and cultural dynamics.[8]

Furthermore, the competitive environment is alive and well in the social sector, albeit sometimes harder to see and masked by an aura of altruism. Nonprofit organizations often work without much general public awareness of their work. They have specific populations they serve and little fanfare about their results. A narrow view of the competitive environment for a new socially entrepreneurial venture can lead a novice to assume "no one is working on this." After some careful analysis, however, the social entrepreneur can determine more clearly who is addressing similar problems and avoid direct competition for scarce resources and undercover potential allies. For example, Steve Rothschild left his position as Executive Vice President of General Mills, where he launched Yoplait, to dig deeply into what Bill George described in his foreword to Steve Rothchild's book, *The Non Nonprofit*[9] as:

> [T]win issues of poverty and racism to see what could be done about them.... His explorations led him to found Twin Cities RISE!. His exploration was based on the bedrock principles of creating value for employers and society to enable the poorest of the poor to qualify for jobs that pay more than $10 per hour.

In his pursuit, Steve encountered entrenched training programs funded by annual government grants and private philanthropy that were not very successful with the hardest to employ. At the same time he found funding policies and government service referral practices had been established that reinforced these approaches and blocked those with new approaches. Steve applied market principles of value creation and return on investment to the design and funding of his new venture. He sought out employers willing to consider hiring Twin Cities RISE! trainees for hard-to-fill jobs. He studied what worked and did not work with other programs, he listened to employers discuss what kept some employees from being successful, and he observed that those he was attempting to serve needed to discover that they needed new skills different from those that allowed them to survive while living in poverty. With that information he designed, tested, and revised his venture.

Longstanding Traditions of Entrepreneurial Creativity in Addressing Social Issues

The phrase social entrepreneurship is relatively new, but the practice of applying creative organization formation to address social issues has a long history. In this context, there are reports of voluntary organizations in ancient Greece, professional organizations and hospitals in ancient Rome, and almshouses in Old England, just to site a few examples. The active pursuit of entrepreneurial solutions to social issues has gone on since the beginning formation of the United States. Benjamin Franklin is praised as the founder of a number of "societies for the general good" including the volunteer fire department and the Library Company in Philadelphia.[10] In the early 20th century, many new organizations emerged to address the fast-growing problems that were side effects of the urbanization caused by the industrial revolution. Too many people flocked to cities while jobs, housing, and other accommodations were not in place. What emerged were creative individuals who acted on their concerns and passions. For example, Hull House in Chicago, founded by Jane Adams and Ellen Starr in 1889, provided a wide range of services to new immigrants and new urbanites teaching English, preaching the dogma of cleanliness, saving, and American cooking.[11]

In the United States, nonprofit organizations have long been sites for diverse ideas and experimentation,[12] innovation,[13] and broader influences on public policy through mobilization of social or economic minorities.[14] Creating new, and hopefully better, approaches to current tough issues is the overall intent of the thousands of newly formed nonprofits each year. Most would be considered socially entrepreneurial ventures. And, with social enterprise, for-profit orientation and thinking have also been added to this mix. Nonprofits in the United States have often relied on social enterprise ventures, embedded profit-generating activities, with a focus on generating revenue to support their underfunded services. For example, the Metropolitan Museum of Art started its first museum-related sales office in 1908.[15] And historically, nonprofits have played important systems-change roles, from framing issues in new ways to getting them into the public's priority-issues agenda, to influencing policymaking itself and monitoring implementation of policy goals.[16]

Internationally, nongovernmental organizations often act as "bridges" between powerful elites and less powerful indigenous communities[17] and, like their US counterparts, are often important for their political, advocacy work. Civil society organizations, a term often used in a global context to include a broader range of activities than nonprofit organizations, have become especially important players in spurring empowerment, stimulating radical change, and battling government corruption and repressive regimes.[18]

Those strong traditions of organized action to address social issues are the general operating environment in which the social entrepreneurs of today operate. Despite our descriptions here of nonprofit and nongovernmental organizations, we do not mean to imply that social ventures only arise in these types of organizations. We agree with Light that the origins and activities of social entrepreneurship can occur in any sector (public, for-profit or nonprofit) and often result in entities with hybrid characteristics from for-profit, public, and/or nonprofit organizations.[19] Indeed, our experiences with students interested in social entrepreneurship (and congruent with those of faculty from other schools, see for example, Ebrahim[20]) suggest that young people are passionate about their ideas and change agendas more than they care about within which "sector" their new organization, project, or program resides. And so this book will include approaches possible in all organizational forms.

Social Entrepreneurs to Learn From

In Table 1.1 you will read about 10 social entrepreneurs whose experiences and results will be used as examples throughout this book.

The Layout of the Book

Throughout the book, we provide conceptual frameworks and specific tools to enable social entrepreneurship practitioners and students to

Table 1.1. Ten Social Entrepreneurs to Learn From

1. Denise DeVaan	Founder, FAIM (see appendix for the full story). Family Assets for Independence in Minnesota works to enable people to escape poverty by changing the assets they own starting with a savings account.[21] For more information about the movement she founded go to http://minnesotafaim.com/index.cfm
2. Jim Frey	President, Frey Family Foundation, systems-change focused philanthropy . For more information on the Frey Foundation visit http://freyfoundationmn.org. (see appendix for the full story)
3. Marion Wright Edelman[22]	Founder, Children's Defense Fund—Since its founding in 1973 CDF has challenged the United States to raise its standards by improving policies and programs for children. It is known for careful research on children's survival, protection and development in all racial and income groups, and for independent analyses of how federal and state policies affect children, their families, and their communities. CDF lets the public know how effectively their elected officials stand up for children. Through this work, they influence the child policy agenda. For more information about the organization and movement she founded go to www. childrensdefense.org
4. Bill Kling	Founder, Minnesota Public Radio (MPR)—Founded in 1967 at Saint John's University in central Minnesota, MPR is now a 42-station regional network providing news as well as classical and contemporary music to over 8 million listeners in the Midwest though traditional radio technology and streaming over the Internet.[23] For more information about the organization visit http://minnesota.publicradio.org
5. Brian Peterson Greg Tehven Irene Fernando Erik Larsen	Founders: Students Today Leaders Forever (STLF)—Founded in 2003, with a mission to reveal leadership through service relationships and action, STLF is engaging college, high school, and middle school students in service and leadership. The Pay It Forward Tour is a dynamic, multiday program focused on service, education, and reflection, during which groups of students travel the country and volunteer in a new city each day. Through Pay It Forward Tours and other programs for middle and high school students, STLF now serves thousands of college, high school, and middle school students of varying demographics by providing opportunities in service and leadership. For more information about the organization visit http://www.stlf.net/home[24]
6. Wendy Kopp	Founder, Teach for America—Since its founding in 1990 nearly 33,000 participants have reached more than 3 million children nationwide during their two-year teaching commitments. They have sustained their commitment as alumni, working within education and across all sectors to help ensure that children growing

(Continued)

Table 1.1. Ten Social Entrepreneurs to Learn From (Continued)

	up in low-income communities get an excellent education. For more information about the movement she founded go to http://www. teachforamerica.org/[25]
7. Steve Rothschild	Founder, Twin Cities RISE!—Founded in 1994 in Minneapolis, MN, RISE! seeks to end concentrated, multigenerational poverty by providing employers with skilled, reliable employees, primarily men of color. For more information about the organization he founded go to http://twincitiesrise.org/[26]
8. Mohammed Yunis	Founder, Grameen Bank—The Grameen Bank project began in Bangladesh in 1983 to help poor people escape from poverty by providing small loans and teaching basic financial principles to enable them to help themselves. The Grameen Bank began a revolution in micro lending, and Yunis was awarded the Nobel Peace Prize in 2006. For more information about the movement he started go to http://www.grameen-info.org/[27]
9. Mike Temali	Cofounder, Neighborhood Development Center (NDC)—Founded in 1993, NDC works with entrepreneurs and community organizations to concentrate the power of micro enterprise development around dynamic "hubs" of community revitalization, linking the energy of people to the vitality of places. This "network of hubs" allows NDC to generate and sustain large-scale impact while communities retain ownership of the process and the results. For more information about Neighborhood Development Center go to http://www.ndc-mn.org. (See appendix for full story)[28]
10. Jacqueline Novogratz	Founder, Acumen Fund—Social Venture philanthropy fund founded in 2001 with seed funding from Rockefeller Foundation, Cisco Foundation, and three other private investors.It supports social entrepreneurs focused on offering critical services—water, health, housing, and energy—at affordable prices to people earning less than four dollars a day. It uses philanthropic capital to make disciplined investments—loans or equity, not grants—that yield both financial and social returns. Any financial returns are recycled into new investments. For more information about the organization she founded go to http://acumen.org/ten/[29]

realistically assess the feasibility of their entrepreneurial idea, identify significant barriers and ways to overcome those barriers, and come to a "go/no go" decision on whether to proceed with in depth venture planning.

The path from passion about an issue to a viable plan of action is not straight. While the sequencing of these chapters can appear to be quite linear, and there is a natural building of information from chapter to chapter, we recognize that many great ideas bear fruit in more circular and unpredictable ways. Most entrepreneurial initiatives, like the entrepreneurs that are driving them forward, are more iterative in nature and are less likely to follow a prescribed path. Indeed, we expect that people will use and reuse the frameworks and tools we present at many junctures in the venture's development. They are not intended to stifle the creative and passionate force that is one of the most vital aspects of success in any social entrepreneurial adventure. Once these tools are applied for a given issue and opportunity, they create a toolkit as well as an analytical process that can be revisited regularly to test modifications of the idea, take advantage of new information about the changing environment, or be applied to a completely new issue.

We begin by introducing an overall model for the social entrepreneurial process of creating a feasible venture plan (Chapter 2). The specific frameworks introduced in the next chapters (Chapters 3–5) take a systematic approach to uncovering key information about the community, policy, and competitive contexts surrounding the issue or idea. In these contexts, undiscovered opportunities for action or major barriers may exist and require a rethinking of ideas. Chapter 3 presents a means to understand the populations to be effected and the ecology of the community in which they live. Chapter 4 focuses on analyzing the policy and political environments surrounding the social entrepreneur's issue. From there, we move in Chapter 5 to a guide for the social entrepreneur to build an understanding of the industry and competitive context. Throughout, we will add specific tools and visual mapping devices for these frameworks that social entrepreneurs can apply directly to their ventures. Chapter 6 brings together the elements that emerge from the work in each of the previous chapters into a venture feasibility plan, and in Chapter 7, we offer a method of reviewing the viability of the social venture framework created.

These frameworks and tools will deepen a social entrepreneur's understanding of the target community, its cultural uniqueness, the competitive, political, and policy landscapes relevant to the issue, and the early venture idea. He will find barriers to progress, overlapping issues needing to be addressed, and attributes of those to be reached that should be considered. The social entrepreneur will discover opportunities, partners, and best approaches to overcome significant barriers that might end up scuttling an otherwise innovative and influential idea.

This book is intended to lead the social entrepreneur from the early stages of issue concern or idea formation through a process of discovery that will result in a feasible venture concept. Whether used as an initial venture feasibility assessment or later, as part of an intensive venture planning process, these tools will produce critical information for success.

CHAPTER 2

Issues, Ideas, and Opportunities—A Simultaneous Pursuit

Rather than leaving societal needs to the government or business sectors, social entrepreneurs find what is not working and solve the problem by changing the system, spreading the solution, and persuading entire societies to take new leaps.

Bill Drayton
Founder/CEO of Ashoka

Learning Goals

1. Understand unique features of issues and ideas in the social entrepreneurship context
2. See how to begin to search for opportunities that join issues and ideas for a new venture concept

When discussing issues, ideas, and opportunities, the social entrepreneurship literature often describes a linear process of moving from issue identification to idea generation to opportunity recognition to venture formation. Arthur Brooks summarizes the process in a series of consecutive steps.[1] Gulclu, Dees, and Anderson of the Center for the Advancement of Social Entrepreneurship describe a step-by-step process that starts with the generation of promising ideas and moves to a step that develops the ideas into promising attractive opportunities.[2]

We have found in undergraduate and graduate classrooms, in our professional philanthropic endeavors, and in issue focused collaborations of community leaders that budding social entrepreneurs of any age are often passionate about either an issue or an idea they have had for some time. We also observed that their actions are not linear. As one social entrepreneur, Tim Reardon, stated recently, "in the early stages it is more like a messy caldron of ideas and concerns, a gurgling mess that defies logical or strict analytical approaches."[3] Upon further reflection, we began to question much of the literature on the early stages of venture creation that describes the process as a linear progression toward the venture framework.

We propose a new model for the social entrepreneurial process that recognizes the social entrepreneur starts with their passion. This passion, regardless of whether it is driven by focus on an issue or an idea, captures their energy better than forcing them to think along more linear lines. We propose that the early stages of social venture creation occur as somewhat independent and interactive streams of exploration that later are connected with opportunities to form a nascent venture.

Issues and Ideas as Independent Streams

We draw on Kingdon's classic work on agenda-setting in the world of policy and politics from which to develop the idea of independent streams.[4] Kingdon argues that three independent processes or streams are in play most of the time in the policy formation process:

1. the problem identification stream that may be stimulated by a crisis or focal event, a change in a major economic or social indicator, etc.;
2. the policy development stream that represents "solutions" to problems and includes the accumulation of knowledge, expertise, and generation of policy alternatives (in other words, the work that "wonks" do); and,
3. the political stream of changes in administrations, Congress, Congressional Committee chairs, etc.

"Windows of opportunity" open, usually in the political stream, which enable the coupling of problems to solutions within a favorable political environment. Policy entrepreneurs are those people who both recognize these "windows" and couple the problems with the solutions/policies. Often, policy entrepreneurs have been working for years in an issue or policy area, waiting for these windows to open wide enough for their intervention.

To translate or modify Kingdon's work for social entrepreneurial purposes, we also see three independent streams: issues, ideas, and opportunities. While we could stress a fairly linear process of moving from issue to idea to opportunity, we instead believe that the generation of issues (like "problems" in Kingdon's framework) and ideas (like "solutions") exist as somewhat separate streams, operating simultaneously with emerging sources of opportunities. It is the social entrepreneur who works to establish the connections. Like the policy entrepreneur, a social entrepreneur recognizes that real opportunities need to be leveraged and coupled with understanding of pressing issues and the strongest innovative ideas. The social entrepreneur understands that you cannot have an identified problem without some concrete ideas for how to solve it and, likewise, it is not enough to have a unique idea or solution without a broader sense of what bigger issue the idea is addressing. Without the coupling you do not get at broader social or economic change. For example, you may have an innovative idea for a new program but without a clearer perspective on what issues/problems it is addressing, the idea becomes a solution in search of a problem. Likewise, you can feel passionately about an issue and actually know quite a bit about the issue, but if you don't have some unique (and also realistic) ideas for how to begin to mitigate the problem/issue, then you have a problem in search of a solution. Even with a focused issue and a developed idea, it is the window of opportunity that provides the impetus for engagement and the access to resources critical to venture framing and eventual launch. Windows of opportunity provide the opportunity to change the status quo.

Issue Discovery

An injustice, a social issue that is not well addressed, or a cause that has affected them personally often first motivate social entrepreneurs. Steve Rothschild, founder of Twin Cities RISE! was passionate about finding ways out of poverty for young adult male African Americans. Wendy Kopp, founder of Teach for America, was passionate about the educational needs of children living in poverty. Denise DeVaan found her passion early in her career as she discovered students in her public school classroom were unable to concentrate because they had not had breakfast and were hungry. That motivation presses the social entrepreneur to find out more about the issue and gives them determination to do something about it. And, it is this passion for a better future for others that sustains the entrepreneur and also motives others to join the endeavor.

Yet, social entrepreneurs often fight a general sense of malaise in others that "this problem will never change." John Skoll who promotes social entrepreneurial action through his Skoll Foundation said in a 2010 speech:

> *The point is that old myths die hard. Even when people have evidence that a myth is untrue, even when they have evidence that it has never been true, it still takes a great deal of time to fade. For much of the past 50 years, there has been a myth perpetrated across the globe that ordinary people cannot change the world.*

He continued,

> *Too many people have come to believe that we can have no discernible effect on the problems that surround us. The media has made people more aware of the issues we face, at the same time that it's brought more attention to the real and perceived failure of big institutions to bring change. That combination has left many people dispirited and cynical. But I know a solution that works every time: I tell people about you. I tell them about Sakena Yacoobi, fighting poverty and warfare in Afghanistan with reading and writing, educating more than 350,000 women and girls each year. I tell them about Martin von Hildebrand and how Gaia Amazonas has helped put nearly 62 million acres of Amazon rainforest in Colombia back into indigenous hands.[5]*

Seeing beyond the despair about an issue requires an intense curiosity. The issue observer must begin to ask why such a thing is occurring. To best understand the issue they ask lots of questions, such as, what is the size and scope of this issue, how many people are affected, what kinds of people, where to do they live, what could change if this issue were addressed? The stage of inquiry about the issue is one that is longer than many action-oriented people may like. It requires a search for facts, interactions with those experiencing the problem, and openness to an array of information. Later chapters will provide the tools to increase the effectiveness of the search for understanding.

Moving from concern to action requires gathering something inside the social entrepreneur as well. As Tim Reardon, a Minneapolis-based social entrepreneur, claims, this move from concern to action requires a strong amount of courage.

It is often in this intersection of an individual's courage and convictions that propel people to exercise leadership and spark the energy to tackle a social issue. It is in this sweet spot that many social change agents have found their motivation to act. It is what propelled Rosa Parks to not take a seat in the back of the bus, Martin Luther King Jr. to lead a bus boycott in Montgomery, led to the burning of bras in the woman's movement in the 1970s, the ACT UP street protests of the 1980s, and the nonviolent protests of the oppressive regime in India led by Gandhi.

Where to start to deepen the understanding of an issue? Often the social issue in focus is one that has many symptoms. This diversity of symptoms can make it difficult to understand where the best entry point for action is. Finding the right trigger or triggers that will cause a domino effect of change is important. Without that search, actions can become responses to symptoms that only cover up the underlying real cause(s) that need to be addressed.

Leadership for change

Figure 2.1. Exercised leadership.
Source: ©Tim Reardon 2013

1. Write down the specific problem
2. Ask WHY the problem happens and write down all the answers
3. Ask WHY again and write down all answers
4. Loop back to step 3 until the team is in agreement that the problem's root cause(s) is identified

This may take fewer or more than five times asking "Why is that?"

Figure 2.2. How to do the five whys with a group.

A group process exercise, "The 5 Why's," helps generate this kind of information by asking a series of "why" questions. The basics of process are asking a series of why questions one after the other. The process was first used by a large automaker in an effort to uncover why manufacturing defaults continued to happen during the production process. Usually those experiencing the issue or engaged in attempts to right the wrong are able to answer "why do you think that is happening?" They will generate many different answers. The group selects one answer that seems to capture the best sense of what is going wrong and then asks again, "why?" might that be the answer. That sets the search path and begins to unveil deeper, contributing causes of the problem or issue.

Take the following example—the issue is "too many 3rd graders are missing days of school."

- 1st Why—Why are 3rd graders missing days of school? Answers: they miss the bus, they are sick too often, they are afraid of someone at school, they have to take care of a younger sibling toddler.
- 2nd Why—Why do children miss the bus? Answers: they don't wake up in time, their parent is off to work before they have to leave for the bus, they don't have warm clothes to wear to wait for the bus, they choose not to go to school, they are sick, etc.
- 3rd Why—Why don't they have warm clothes? Answers: their parents have poverty-level incomes, they are new refugees and did not anticipate needing such warm clothes
- 4th Why—Why aren't warm clothes and an introduction to coping with cold weather given to new arriving refugees? Answers: refugee

service organizations don't have enough donated clothes to give, nor funds to purchase such expensive items

- 5th Why—Why do so many in Minnesota have extra winter coats their children have grown out of and these children go without coats? Answer: there is no concerted effort to get these items donated, no easy way to donate and no system to collect and distribute them

It is this concluding discovery that spurred a group of Minnesotans to launch "donate a coat" campaign.

This process of questioning does a number of things. First it helps subdivide the target population into categories. In this example, new immigrants needing cold weather clothes require a very different solution than do those children whose parents are not at home when they must leave for the bus. The first group may need a solution of donated winter clothing, while the second may need multiple strategies including an unusual approach such as an alarm clock or a different school start time that is earlier so most working parents are still home when they leave.

The process also points to areas needing further fact gathering. For example, does research exist that suggests these "causes" are linked to the central problem that has been identified? Are there other factors involved that the group has not considered? What can people experiencing the issue tell about it and its causes? What issue experts might be tapped to help confirm, modify, expand or even reject the thinking that the group has just completed? In Chapters 3 and 4 we present processes and information analysis that will guide the social entrepreneur through this process of deeper investigation of the issue.

Seeing Possibilities—Idea Generation

Bill Drayton, CEO of Ashoka, focuses the work of his organization on the person who sees the issue solution and is so driven to change a problem that they are not satisfied until they have changed how society functions. "Social entrepreneurs often seem to be possessed by their ideas, committing their lives to changing the direction of their field. They are both visionaries and ultimate realists, concerned with the practical implementation of their vision above all else."[6]

Innovative thinking is a skill that is very helpful for idea generation. Innovation is interlinked with an understanding of what change is. Idea generation that is framed in innovative thinking can result in a list of important ideas. Erica Swallow, a contributor to Forbes magazine, in April 2012 summarized the most recent work on innovation thinking:

> But are some of us born innovators and the rest of us just hopeless? Hal Gregersen, senior affiliate professor of leadership at INSEAD and co-author of *The Innovator's DNA*, believes that there are five key skills that disruptive innovator's possess: the cognitive skill of associating and the behavioral skills of questioning, observing, networking, and experimenting. And yes, all of us can learn to flex these innovator's muscles, Gregersen told me in a recent interview.[7]

Gregersen and coauthors Clayton M. Christensen (professor of business administration at the Harvard Business School) and Jeff Dyer (professor of strategy at Brigham Young University's Marriott School) believe that roughly two-thirds of the skills it takes to innovate can be learned. In their own research involving hundreds of innovators and thousands of entrepreneurs, managers, and executives from around the world, Gregersen, Christensen, and Dyer boiled the formula of innovation down to five key skills:

- **Questioning** allows innovators to challenge the status quo and consider new possibilities;
- **Observing** helps innovators detect small details—in the activities of customers, suppliers, and other companies—that suggest new ways of doing things;
- **Networking** permits innovators to gain radically different perspectives from individuals with diverse backgrounds;
- **Experimenting** prompts innovators to relentlessly try out new experiences, take things apart and test new ideas;
- **Associational thinking**—drawing connections among questions, problems or ideas from unrelated fields—is triggered by questioning, observing, networking and experimenting and is the catalyst for creative ideas.

Generating ideas should also be the approach for social entrepreneurs and using the same techniques Gregersen and Christensen identified works for idea generation for social solutions. Unfortunately, we have experienced frequently that some novice social entrepreneurs "fall in love" with their first idea and do not think about other possible innovative approaches. A much better process is to generate several ideas which the social entrepreneur can then evaluate and select the best approach.

Finding Opportunities

Entrepreneurs see change as the norm and as healthy. Usually, they don't bring about the change themselves. But—and this defines an entrepreneur and entrepreneurship—*the entrepreneur always searches for change, responds to it, and exploits it as an opportunity.*

Innovation is the specific tool of entrepreneurs, the means by which they exploit change and opportunity for a different business or different service. It is capable of being presented as a discipline, capable of being learned, capable of being practiced. Entrepreneurs need to search purposefully for the sources of innovation, the changes and their symptoms that indicate opportunities for successful innovation.[8]

Peter Drucker wrote this description nearly 30 years ago about the practice and discipline of innovation in his book *Innovation and Entrepreneurship.*[9] In that book he lays out how to practice seeing innovation all around and how that leads to the practice of entrepreneurship.

Social entrepreneurs can use Drucker's sources of innovation as a set of lenses to look for opportunities to couple their issues with innovative ideas or solutions. They are areas where change is occurring, where the "status quo" may no longer operate, similar to Kingdon's windows of opportunity. For the social entrepreneur, a changing environment and a disruption of the status quo provides an opening for action to capture growing interest in an issue and gather support to implement an innovative solution.

Drucker described seven sources of change that we have adapted to the context of social entrepreneurship. These sources of change all provide areas where the social entrepreneur can identify opportunities that can be exploited with innovation ideas to address an issue of concern.

1. **The unexpected change:** a surprising success or failure. These events are often overlooked by service sector leaders, civic leaders, and elected officials who are focused elsewhere and mostly on sustaining the status quo or implementing the plan as designed. However, when an unexpected success, failure, or event occurs, it is often a symptom of some change that is occurring and an emerging opportunity.

   A social entrepreneur can ask "what basic change is happening that is being overlooked? And how can I use that change to further my cause?" Is there an opportunity to "go with the flow" and insert ideas for action with this change momentum? For example, a social entrepreneur focused on addressing the lack of education advancement for autistic children may see the unexpected or novel use of personal technology. When autistic children began to use iPads in their homes and suddenly were communicating more with those around them, educators heard about it and added iPads to their work with the children. The result is changing how education happens with autistic children. Thus an opportunity was observed, influenced an idea and an issue, and a new action was implemented.[10]

2. **The incongruity:** An incongruity is a disconnect between what actually is and what is assumed or "ought to be." These reflect a change within an industry, a market or a process or a misunderstanding about the customer or client. In the social sector "what ought to be" is often framed in the values of the dominant culture. That can become blinders to change. In the offering of a current product or service there are practices that become refined and routine, yet a change in demand type, volume, or location can significantly impact the "we have always done it that way" practice. Even in new product or service designs there are assumptions or educated guesses about what the customer wants. Watching for these incongruities can be a way to identify opportunities to initiate innovation.

   A social entrepreneur can ask "what is the customer's behavior telling us about their needs and preferences?" For example, a program designed to help low-income people begin to save offered a 2:1 match for every dollar they saved. Encouragement to save even $10 included various additional incentives, yet some people did not go to the bank to begin the process. Investigations into why that was happening uncovered that people often did not have bank experience and were afraid of banks. Beginning a program to teach low-income people how to use banks and to teach bankers how to best interact with these people resulted in new bank customers.[11]

3. **Innovation based on process need**: Opportunities can be found in seeking areas of weakness in funding streams, current standard social practices, policy systems, or service delivery processes. These can be observed as a weak link, an out-of-date application of knowledge technology, or one where a new constituent group does not respond the same as other groups. Those delivering the services everyday may readily identify the need for process improvements. A social entrepreneur can ask, "what about this process is keeping those I am concerned about from getting what they need? What additions can be made to a process change underway that would affect the issue and population I am concerned about? Is there an opportunity here to implement one of my ideas?"

4. **Change in industry or market sector**: This area of opportunity occurs when there is a change that catches everyone unaware and unravels the operating practice of a whole industry. For example, when customers switched from using newspaper want ads to sell used "stuff" to posting it on a web-based listing at eBay, Craigslist, etc., it took the newsprint industry by surprise and significantly impacted their revenue. Sometimes this kind of change is just about very rapid growth that exceeds the capacity of an industry to respond. In the social sector it can be a major change in regulation or a shift in funding focus. This kind of change triggers what some may call chaos in the industry that at the same time creates significant opportunities for new idea implementation.

5. **Demographics**: Changes in population, its size, age structure, income and educational level, economic level, racial composition, can be both predictable and unpredictable. All of these kinds of changes are opportunities.

   Social entrepreneurs are often the first to respond to these kinds of opportunities as they are often the first to see the issues faced by the new demographics. Social entrepreneurs are able to develop new forms of responses quickly and the opportunity created by this demographic change can stimulate a welcoming response by others already operating in that industry or system.

6. **Changes in human perception, mood, or meaning:** When perception changes in the general population, they can become opportunities to act for a social entrepreneur. When this kind of change happens, the facts about an issue do not change, but their meaning to the public does. Public values about the issue may be changing and creating a new willingness to embrace an idea that previously was rejected. This change can open doors to new innovations and at the same time can also turn against traditional approaches another window of opportunity.

   Social entrepreneurs can help make this kind of change happen if they focus the action strategies on changing attitudes or public will.

7. **New Knowledge:** The introduction of new knowledge to a field creates significant streams of new opportunities. This kind of change usually has the longest lead time but still can be one ignored by the current systems. Drucker says,

   There is, first, a long time span between the emergence of new knowledge and its becoming applicable to technology. And then there is another long period before the new technology turns into products, processes, or services in the market place.

Social entrepreneurs can miss knowing about the newest knowledge that could improve their approaches to problems. The new knowledge is often not promoted in media reaching social entrepreneurs. New research on human behaviors, new health research, and new technology that could have life improving advantages for those served are often only found in professional journals. As a result, change inside the social sector can lag behind market place focused change. At the same time those who are deeply engaged in applications of new knowledge may tap into their own experiences of issues and create new ideas for application of their new knowledge or technology.

Initiating all Three Streams

We believe that a social entrepreneur needs skills related to understanding and analyzing all three streams described in this chapter.

1. Issue: Determining the focal issue or problem area is a key part of the social entrepreneurial process. At the beginning, one problem area

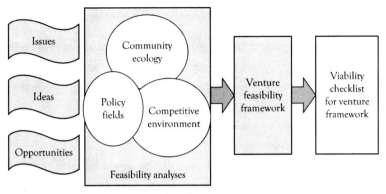

Figure 2.3. Organizing framework.

may seem dominant, but as the social entrepreneur continues to develop the venture, he or she may grow to understand that several problem areas are tightly interrelated and must be understood both separately and together.

2. Ideas: Having a working list of possible ideas for action on the issue is a second key part of a venture approach. Keeping a list of them and revisiting them regularly as new information comes to light are key parts of the venture development process.

3. Opportunities: Opportunities in the social and public sectors are changes in the environment that allow for the entrance of a new idea or approach. Determining the most likely sources of opportunities is a critical third area for attention for a social entrepreneur. Opportunities happen all the time. So monitoring sources for opportunity is part of the ongoing work of a social entrepreneur.

Figure 2.3 illustrates how independent streams of issues, ideas, and opportunities come together for deeper connections through a series of important analytical processes (Chapters 3, 4, and 5). The result is the beginning of a feasible venture framework that has an overall vision, clear statement of the problems to be solved and innovative ideas for solving it, and anticipated results (Chapter 6). The viability check (Chapter 7) summarizes a final assessment by the social entrepreneur of whether the venture is a viable approach, ready for further development and resource support.

Venture Development Questions

1. Write a 1–2 paragraphs describing the issue as you understand it now.
2. How is the population of interest impacted by the issue?
3. Describe at least 3 ideas that could be implemented to address the issue.
4. Identify where you will look to discover opportunities that could be tied to the ideas and issues.
5. Describe what aspects of an opportunity would be most important for your venture.

CHAPTER 3

Understanding Those to Be Served and Their Communities

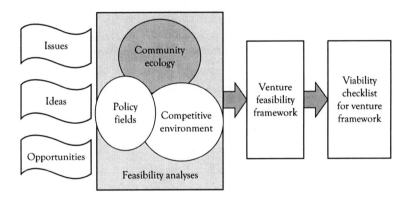

There are two ways of being creative. One can sing and dance. Or one can create an environment in which singers and dancers flourish.

Warren G. Bennis

Learning Goals

1. Develop deeper understanding of the target population to be effected by the social venture.
2. Understand the community environment of the forces for and against change.
3. Understand specific population and community-based aspects of the issue.

Arthur Brooks in *Social Entrepreneurship* says that the knowledge an entrepreneur has about the population to be served is crucial to successful creation of new social value.[1] It is that knowledge that sets the stage for bright ideas, the something new that can stimulate the desired change.

The action of moving between issue and idea and linking to a good opportunity that can result in a viable venture concept requires two simultaneous discovery processes:

1. The idea is determined to be possible to do in the given setting
2. It is determined that the population to be reached is willing and able to connect to the idea.

In a market-driven process, this would be described as "supply and demand" match. In social entrepreneurial processes, it is sometimes called the "social value proposition" which is the expected impact of a proposed venture on society that is achieved by fulfilling an unmet social need.[2]

The task at this stage is to find where the idea for action on the issue matches what the target population wants or needs. In many cases, the best a social entrepreneur can do is to determine that the service, action, or product has high potential to be what the target population wants or needs.

Choosing which idea(s) to pursue to drive the change desired must be informed by an understanding of the target population. For a purely business venture this group of people would be called the target market. To understand them, the business entrepreneur may use surveys, interviews, focus groups and more to inform the selection of strategies that will be of interest or meet the need of a specific customer.

In the social sector, this kind of information collection can also be helpful and may be included in an overall information collection plan. But there are many other factors that must be taken into account in addition to the specific interests and desires of a target market. Economic status, family status, life experiences, education level, and culture all add to a deepened understanding of those who are intended to benefit. While surveying the prospective target beneficiaries can assess the relevance of a perceived need, Kickul and Lyons caution "target beneficiaries' responses to anything that may be of benefit to them tend to be skewed to the positive."[3] That information is only part of what is needed to guide the choices about the best approaches to take.

More broadly, the goal of the information collection strategy presented in this chapter is to provide a strong understanding of the context of the issue to be addressed. Gathering information about the target population and the community in which they live is critical to a successful opportunity selection process. As Brooks argues, gathering this kind of information is a key part of the background necessary for the creative process of generating ideas and opportunities.[4]

While many successful social entrepreneurs reach to their own life and work experience and tap into their social networks to start building understanding of target populations, a new social entrepreneur may be starting from little experience so this information collection becomes critical. In either case these early notions must be augmented by conscientious information gathering process. Both experienced and new entrepreneurs benefit from close attention to understanding those they expect to impact.

Understanding the Target Population

The target population is a group of people that are the intended beneficiaries of the social entrepreneurial venture. A target population is described by what the people have in common. It can be described by demographic characteristics, common behaviors, common problems, illnesses, geographic area of residence, etc. Target populations can also be selected for their common psychographics such as attitudes, lifestyle choices, or life experiences.

Some ventures have more than one target population and will modify the action strategies to accommodate the differences. Some ventures have primary target populations and secondary ones. For example, a program to improve academic achievement of elementary school aged children will often have a secondary target population that includes the parents of those children or those who teach them. Strategies to reach their distinct but interconnected needs make for a stronger venture with increased likelihood of success.

A target population or target beneficiaries are different from a target market in a profit driven venture.

Target Market in a Profit Driven Venture

This is a group of people that the venture has selected to target with its marketing efforts. The venture may or may not modify its product or service to match the specific needs of that target market. A measure of success in this kind of venture is that the people in the target market purchase the product or service and become loyal customers. There is a direct interaction between the target market and the venture itself often measured by the price paid for the product and the volume of purchases.[5]

Target Market in a Social Entrepreneurial Venture
Becomes a Target Population

In a social entrepreneurial venture, the target population describes the people who are expected to have changed behaviors and/or changed lives as a result of the venture. Those individuals may or may not purchase the product or service directly. Often the product or service may be subsidized by resources from others, including donors, foundations, or governments.

Target Beneficiaries

For some social entrepreneurial ventures there is no direct interaction with those who benefit the most. When a well is installed in a community without access to fresh water or when a solar energy field brings electricity to a community, only the local elected officials may be directly engaged, not those who will benefit over the long term. So the phrase "target beneficiaries" is often used to describe the people whose lives will change from these kinds of social entrepreneurial ventures.

For simplicity purposes we will use the phrase target population for target population and target beneficiaries here after. The selection of the target populations often requires difficult decisions about who to begin reaching and for whom the service will be delayed for some period of time. A target population may include any of the following:

1. The population easiest to reach
2. The population most likely to change in the shortest time

3. The population experiencing the most difficult aspects of the issue or problem in focus

Why Understanding a Target Community Is Important

When selecting a population to target, the social entrepreneur must also take into consideration the community in which those people live, work, and socialize. The differences in community experiences within a target population can be wide ranging. An understanding of the community in which the initial population to be reached enhances the choices of approach. That community becomes the target community.

Community psychologists believe that the problem an individual experiences is defined always with awareness of the person's environment and their own adaption to it and the specific circumstances in the ecosystem in which the person functions.[6] Sometime viable approaches focus on the individual, but more often approaches focus on community strategies in combination with products and services directed to individuals.

Ideas generated to address an issue often include community wide strategies. Creating a community that effectively cares for all its members is a dream of many individuals and is the mission of many social institutions. Time, money, group efforts, and more are pulled together and directed at problems that affect community members. Institutions are called upon to lead an army of resources to "attack" complex community problems. Yet what it takes to resolve community problems is too often seen as a mystery. Without an understanding of how the community works, the chances of success are less.

Knowing how a community functions, how its various members take on roles and assign responsibilities, determining what roles are played by various institutions, and understanding how community change happens will improve the effect of those directed actions. Better results are likely if actions are targeted to areas that block change or are ready for change.

Building Knowledge About the Target Community

Understanding the target community includes understanding how the social systems and institutional infrastructures engage with the target population. This is crucial information for the ultimate selection of the best strategies. Understanding how a community functions requires bringing together information about individual behavior, social practice, institutional behaviors, cultural attributes, and the government policies that can encourage or block success. Without that information, the choice of approach has much higher risk of failure.

A target community is often a geographic community. The geographic boundaries of a target community are determined by the homogeneity of the environment and the community factors. In some cities for some issues, the social interactions and resources available to residents vary by neighborhood, so the target community would be a specific neighborhood. For other social issues, there is a uniformity of interactions and resources for the whole urban area. For example, food deserts have distinct geographic boundaries identified by the distance a resident is able or willing to travel to obtain food for themselves and their families. A target community for an unemployment issue analysis may be determined by the area where most unemployed live and by the reach of public transportation available to them. A target community for a K-12 education issue action is most often framed by the boundaries of the school district.

There are target communities that are widely dispersed. For example, people with a specific chronic disease may be widely dispersed across many states. Still those individuals have much experience in common that should be understood by the social entrepreneur.

A tool to sort the information was designed by Terri Barreiro in her work to assist United Way volunteers do planning for the best use of funds raised by that organization.[7] The Community Ecosystems Circles Model provides a way to visualize the complex social systems that are at work in any given community. It identifies dominant institutions, it frames the interaction between elements of that community, it points to where social norms, community practices and laws are set, and it provides a way to focus on the best chances for change.

A social entrepreneur can use this framework to combine deeper understanding of the issue in focus with a deeper understanding of what might work best within the target community.

Using Ecology Principles to Understand Large Groups of Humans

The concept of community ecosystem is borrowed from biologists and ecologists who focus on the community of living organisms (plants, animals, and microbes) in conjunction with the nonliving components of their environment (things like air, water, and mineral soil), interacting as a system. First used for family systems thinking by Urie Bronfenbrenner,[8] a human community as ecosystem framework has also been used by the business community. James F. Moore wrote about it in the *Harvard Business Review* in May/June 1993 defining "business ecosystem" as:

> *An economic community supported by a foundation of interacting organizations and individuals—the organisms of the business world. The economic community produces goods and services of value to customers, who are themselves members of the ecosystem. The member organisms also include suppliers, lead producers, competitors, and other stakeholders.*

The Community Ecosystem Model is a reflection of a social community. Its structure will change depending on the social cultural context of the community. We will primarily use a description of the model as seen for a typical United States urban community to introduce it.

The diagram presents a view of the various elements of a complex human community ecosystem. Social practices, structures, and institutions all play roles that support or limit individual and family members of a community. By understanding the roles and interplay of these various institutions, those working to address an issue can improve the chances for success and expand on the community capacity to meet the needs of all citizens.

There are common, socially reinforced roles that people take on. For example, families often play significant roles in addressing an issue that is experienced by one or more of its members. When a child struggles in school, parents may increase the time they spend at home helping the child understand their homework assignment and encourage the child to do his or her homework. In a family where there is only one parent, the time available for this kind of attention to the child can be limited. In a family where English is not spoken at home assistance in understanding the homework may not be possible. Knowing the underlying family structure predominant in a given community helps set priorities among the ideas for action that a social entrepreneur has identified.

In any community there are formal and informal social networks that add to the resources an individual or family can turn to when in need. Extended family, friends, and neighbors are often those first turned to. Neighborhood-based resources, such as a local church may be the next to get an inquiry for help.

Using Community Ecosystem thinking also helps a social entrepreneur to gather the information about what these resources are for a target population. It also helps identify where a lack of resources may be the barrier to progress. It helps to identify potential partners and reveals opportunities. And finally this information gathering can help point to potential best avenues for actions.

The Community Ecosystem Model is depicted as a series of concentric circles (Figure 3.1). The diagram shows this interplay between the individual and those around him or her. For simplicity of visualization an individual is in the middle surrounded by the various circles of influence on them. Those circles also show the distance the institutions have from the individual and the roles those institutions play when they are healthy

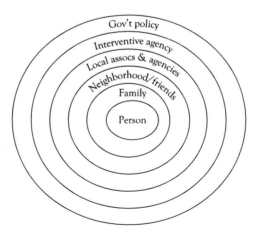

Figure 3.1. Circles of support: Understanding a community ecosystem.

and effectively engaged. Each ring in the diagram can generate possible strategies needed to resolve identified issues.

The Center

This is the individual. It should be noted that in the case of children, the child and the adult(s) who are totally dedicated to their nurturing are in the center. Bronfenbrenner first introduced this ecosystem model with a child focus in mind. When assessing the need of the individual in focus possible strategies can be identified just by better understanding that person. For example, improving the skills of the individual to face life's challenges on their own may be needed. Opportunities for positive impact on the issue in focus often include direct interaction with individuals. Direct assistance or education and training offered to individuals may be the best or at least one of the necessary strategies. If all other aspects of a community are working well then this may be the only action needed.

Family Ring of Support

The family (in its broadest definition), when functioning well, is committed to the healthy growth and development of its individual members. Cultural variations in the roles and responsibilities of family members influence how this ring of support affects the problem. Improving the family's skills and capacity to support its members may be needed and may be the best approach. The economic status of the family and the other issues the family is facing need to be taken into account when designing opportunities for family impact.

For example, action strategies can focus on the family by providing training for improved interaction, adding products to the household, stabilizing the length of time they live in the same home, or building knowledge in the family about the issue and how to counteract it.

Friends' and Neighbors' Ring of Support

Sometimes the help of close friends and neighbors is needed to face life's challenges or to improve skills. These are people that families and individuals feel they can call on often and in a crisis. Equipping these individuals to be successful in the assistance they give can be effective parts of strategies selected. Expanding this network of support for individuals and families is also sometimes needed. Cultural differences in size and influence of this group should be considered as solutions are suggested.

Community/Neighborhood Institutions of Support

Churches, synagogues and mosques, schools, YMCAs, YWCAs, Scouts, community centers, and even the local retailer all provide more formal ways for individuals and families to regularly connect with others and to learn, grow and meet their own variety of needs for living. Assessing the prevalence of these important institutions as well as assessing what they may have contributed to the problem is a critical step in selecting the right mix of strategies to address an issue. Institutions may need to be created, expanded, strengthened, or updated to meet the needs of those they should be supporting. Understanding the cultural variations in the roles played by various institutions is essential to successful problem solving.

Professional and Interventive Services

Hospitals, counseling services, chemical dependency treatment centers, foster homes, and courts are examples of needed professional services. These institutions step in when the help needed is beyond the skills of a layperson or a community organization. Some communities do not have the necessary interventive services available to them. Others may have an overabundance of these services, which then can become overused to the detriment of the family and community. An assessment of the strengths and weaknesses of the professional and interventive institutions accessible to the target audience will enhance the knowledge needed to determine the best set of strategies to address an issue.

Policy Support

Governments set policies that direct and set limitations on how institutions operate. Policies define how the various circles of support interact with one another and ultimately support the individual and family.

Sometimes policies need to be set or changed to improve how the individual and family are supported. Public policy also defines community standards for how individuals are expected to relate to one another. These may also need to be changed. Chapter 4 provides a guide for analyzing the policy contours of an issue and a means to assess ideas to determine the best opportunities for impact.

Public Values and Will

General public values create an atmosphere within which all these community ecology elements function. Prejudices, biases, myths, and cultural folklore are all part of the ecosystem that needs to be studied. These public attitudes are informed and reflected through the media, community dialogue, etc. Public will can encourage or discourage new approaches. Sometimes a strategy needs to be added to the approach to provide the general public new information, reminders of facts, or tools to debunk myths.

Gathering the Necessary Information; Doing the Research

Once an issue has been identified, a general target population has been selected and an array of ideas have been drafted it is time to study the community within which the target population functions.

Interviewing those living or working in the community or those who have studied it can be a way to gather important information. Appreciative Inquiry is a form of inquiry that works well in these kinds of information gathering processes as it starts with asking about the positives. David Cooperrider of Case Western Reserve University developed this method for use in organizational development in the mid-1980s. Appreciative Inquiry is a guided exploration of where an organization, a population or community is, wants to be and dreams to be. It concludes with specific statements that are grounded in the real experience and personal history.[9] More can be found about this tool at www.appreciativeinquiry.case.edu.

Other steps to be taken include reading local newspapers or news websites as well as more traditional research literature searches.

As you frame a plan to collect the necessary information, it is best to determine what is critical to your future understanding of the target population and the ecosystem around it for the specific issue in focus. Key questions should guide this information gathering for each ring in the model:

1. How is that segment of the ecosystem impacted by the issue?
2. What does this segment of the ecosystem contribute to the issue? What attributes about this segment blocks progress?
3. What does or could this segment of the ecosystem contribute to solutions. What resources does it have? What assets and resources exist that can be redirected for action on the issue?
4. What actions are easiest for that segment to undertake?

Figure 3.2 reflects what the discussion of one issue can uncover when the social ecology model provides focus.

Often during the information collection process and in interviews of larger group discussions there is a request for additional facts that are not readily available. Sometimes the best approach for this collection of important information is to make it part of the set of strategies selected to implement in the social entrepreneurial venture.

Awareness of important available resources for implementation often emerges during this process as well. A quick mapping of resources can help to see where strategies may need to be focused and where possible resources and partners may be found. Figure 3.3 shows resources that could be applied to addressing school success in a specific community.

Partnering for Greater Impact

When a community ecosystem model is completed, a new understanding of the target community and its behaviors around an issue is formed. In addition a new set of partner resources can also be discovered. Local communities often have an array of institutional resources that can be recruited for action. Those resources can be recruited to join in the efforts to be launched or recognized as available relieving the necessity of initiating a needed action.

Impact of issue on segment (1)	Contribution to issue (2)	Resources that could be used (3)	Possible strategies easiest to undertake (4)
Individual: - Drops out - Drawn to crime - No HS diploma - ADHD not treated	- Poor learning skills - No passing grades - Poor attendance - Lack of hope for future	- Sports skills motivation - Job motivation - Untapped artistic talents	- Give alarm clock to improve attendance - Offer Incentives for achievement - Test for adhd
Family - Frustration - Defensiveness	- Single parent often - Low income - Limited English	- Parental pride - Need for $$ - Home feels safe - Values education	- Home based tutoring - Parenting education - Free computer & internet access
Friends/ Neighbors - Crime victims - Also drop outs	- Neighbors dont know each others kids - Fear caused isolation	- Use church link - Families stay many years - Older residents need things to do	- Start block clubs for parents and neighbors - Engage churches
Local Community - Idle youth - Rising crime - Schools overwhelmed	- Schools lack staffing - Few afterschool services - No organized local sports	- Dedicated teachers - Public parks underused - Active churches - New YMCA to open - Grocery is locally owned	- Start alternative school - Organize local sports teams at parks - Engage local business owners as tutors
Interventive Services High demand	- Courts not prosecuting truancy	- After school tutors looking for new space - Strong Big Brothers Big Sisters organization - Adult CD treatment center near by	- Add staff to schools and courts - Focus BBBS on this community
Public Policy Pressure on courts	- Unclear rules about truancy - Police have no relationship	- Truancy laws in place - Police officers with some extra time - Mayor launched jobs for youth program	- Advocate for truancy law training
Public Will - focused on crimes - negative attitude about youth	- Little attention to teens	- Local radio & TV stations looking for upbeat stories - New alternative school legislation with funding	- "All kids deserve many chances" education campaign

Figure 3.2. Issue: Too many children are dropping out of school in a poverty-stricken area of the city and too many are not completing high school.

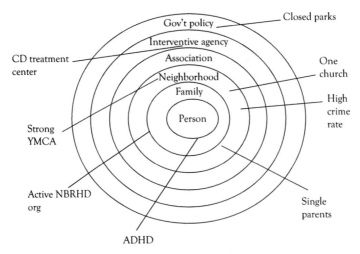

Figure 3.3. Ecosystem snapshot: School success resources and barriers.

Following is the list that shows the kinds of resources that can be identified while doing a community assessment. During the community information collection process attention should be given to finding these kinds of services.

Educational Programs, Information, and Referral Services

These kinds of services provide individuals, families, or neighbors the information they need about an issue and details about how to connect with existing community services or Interventive services. If such services are not available extra work may be needed to ensure this information is collected and available. Enabling the individual to change themselves along with informal assistance around them can be good solution for a portion of the target population.

Existing Institutions and Services

As the community information collection focuses on this circle more in-depth information may be needed. This tally could include: where existing services are, what they do, any admission requirements, facilities, fees and some information about service quality such as customer reviews. Names, areas of expertise, and contact information are also critical. Once you know the services that are currently available for individuals and families the social entrepreneur may be able to use their space, talents, administrative services, and more to reduce program costs and increase impact. In addition this information defines the local "industry" that the social entrepreneur will be operating within.

New Program Host Possibilities

Sometimes the best solution is a new program model that does not exist in the community. Sometimes a local social service is willing to take on the role of home base for the effort.

Research Sources

Sometimes additional more in-depth information or research is needed. Local government offices, higher education institutions, United Ways, Community Foundations or city, county or state governments are good places to contact to determine if the needed information is already available or they can be encouraged to can do added research.

Public Awareness Education

What institutions are ones that are trusted by the community as an information source? What public information has been given to the community about this issue? Often the community is not aware of the scope or seriousness of the issue or that there are solutions. Partnering with a respected organization that is the expert at getting the attention of the total community can be instrumental in creating momentum to act on the issue.

Ecosystems Can Vary Widely from Community to Community and from Culture to Culture

As we said earlier the tool is introduced here with a United States urban community in mind. The ecosystem framework itself changes depending on the kind of community in focus. The first aspect of community to understand is to determine what elements are in a specific community ecosystem. The array of elements and their interrelationship should reflect the actual ecological environment of the society. Within a given society or social group the elements of the ecosystem tend to be similar in their role and in the relationships among them. But between different societies or social groups the constituents' ecosystems can vary markedly. These unique ecosystem distinctions can easily be found between social classes, ethnic and religious groups and entire societies.[10]

Cultures have significant variations in how a community ecosystem functions. Staff from the United Way of Halifax created a version of the basic template to better reflect the First Nation communities they work with in Nova Scotia, shown in figure 3.4. Here the family is the core, and the individual is always considered within the family context. Instead of the friends and local neighborhoods elements of the ecosystem it is the nation or tribe itself that plays both roles in these tight knit communities. Any social entrepreneurial venture would need to gain support and a strong relationship with the nation and its leadership. In this case the information collected would be sorted differently to reflect the community ecosystem reflected below.

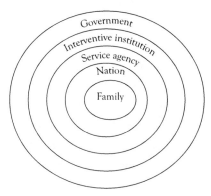

Figure 3.4. Illustration: Community ecosystem map adapted for first nations in Nova Scotia.

Summary

This chapter challenges the social entrepreneur to engage deeply with the populations to be served and to build an understanding of how the community in which they live operates. It guides the social entrepreneur to assess the social ecosystem of the target community. It argues that understanding the interactions between those to be directly reached and those around them is integral in affecting long-term change. It argues that the social entrepreneur can better focus strategy selection after taking on this study and analysis. And it provides a visual framework, Figure 3.1, that is easy to use in summarizing that analysis.

Venture Development Questions

1. What are the specific important aspects of your target population and target community?
2. What are positive forces in the community?
3. What are barriers to progress in the community?
4. Identify possible allies and partners that are in the community?
5. How might the written Issue statement need to be revised?
6. What opportunities have been discovered during this information collection and analysis?

CHAPTER 4

The Policy Environment— Opportunities and Constraints

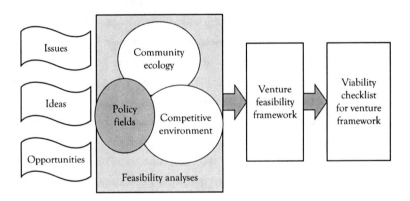

"*I founded RISE! to combat poverty in the Twin Cities. But before I could do that, I had to learn about poverty in the United States...After three decades of spending federal and private money on this issue, why had it grown worse and not better? I decided to find out.*"

Steve Rothschild[1]

Learning Goals

1. Understand why it is essential to assess local, state, and national policy environments to sharpen issue definition.
2. Understand and apply policy field analysis tools in order to discern public policy windows of opportunity, barriers, funding sources, and potential allies.

Overview of Policy Field Analysis

Much like industry or competitor analysis illuminates opportunities and barriers that are rooted in industry structure and market forces (see Chapter 5), policy fields analysis focuses on those aspects of the institutional and public policy environments that may present opportunities and constraints for the venture concept. As discussed earlier, the social entrepreneur often has a passionate commitment to attacking an important public problem or an idea for a venture that she or he thinks will solve that problem. Nearly all of these issues and ideas touch on public policies, perhaps even laws, regulations, and funding streams, aimed at addressing aspects of the issue or idea. Therefore, it is critically important that the social entrepreneur, early in the venture's development, become familiar with the contours of the policy environment surrounding the problem the social entrepreneur wants to solve. It is likely that many institutional and non institutional actors, such as government agencies, local nonprofit organizations, and informal coalitions, are already involved in the general problem area. For example, government agencies are involved directly in implementing poverty reduction programs and also contract with local nonprofits to provide services as well. Other nonprofits, coalitions, or partnerships may be active advocating for changes in poverty reduction policies at state and national levels or may be pushing for changes in how policy makers and the public define and understand poverty as it relates to racial and gender differences.

A policy field analysis, therefore, is especially useful to sharpen the definition of what issue or problem the venture concept is attempting to solve because it deepens social entrepreneurs' understanding of the relevant policy and political contexts. A policy field analysis will also help social entrepreneurs refine how they frame the issue, see other issues or problems to which it is related, and enable social entrepreneurs to identify resources and engage with experts and potential collaborators.

A policy field analysis is a framework that helps the social entrepreneur systematically understand who key stakeholders are and what kinds of power and resources they have. Policy fields are federal, state, and local structures of roles and relationships among people, organizations, and institutions in a substantive policy area in a particular place.[2] This definition is pretty abstract but if we take the example of the need for more high quality and accessible early childhood education, we can make it more concrete.

The policy field of early childhood education is fragmented, siloed, and very complex with significant variations from state to state.[3] For example, in Minnesota, early childhood education services are offered by Head Start agencies, nonprofit and private preschools and child care centers, licensed homes, local churches, and public schools. Funding for these services comes from multiple sources including the federal government (for Head Start), a voucher-like subsidy offered by the state of Minnesota's Child Care Assistance Program (which in turn gets its funding from both federal and state sources), and local philanthropic sources, including an array of private foundations, the United Way, and one foundation created by private business leaders. Parents pay some portion of the costs as well, based on their ability to pay. Local counties administer the Child Care Assistance Program through contracts with regional nonprofit childcare resource and referral agencies. School districts implement school readiness and parent education programs. Various nonprofit advocacy groups exist to influence public policy, especially concerning public funding to those in need, while other small associations represent particular interests in the field, such as family day care providers. A national accreditation body, the National Association for the Education of Young Children, has established standards that allow providers to receive higher rates once they are accredited. The University of Minnesota also has faculty and centers that conduct research and engage with providers of early childhood education within its College of Education and Human Development.

What we see from this example are both public and private sources of funding which are likely to come with important but different requirements. Public funding is also likely to come with some mandates and regulations concerning aspects of the particular early childhood education program. We also see some networks of relationships that are relatively formal through, for example, government grants for Head Start providers and county contracts with regional nonprofit child care programs. On the other hand, many networks within policy fields emerge more informally through the development of working relationships and the formation of coalitions as people and organizations work together to implement and/

or change public policy approaches and goals.[4] We also see that there are research resources through the University and private research organizations that can be tapped for additional information.

Put more generally, policy fields both shape the roles and relationships in policy systems and are shaped by them. It is very important to understand this duality—a social entrepreneur confronts existing relationships, rules, resource flows, and even values and norms that structure how people think about and try to solve the issue that concerns the social entrepreneur, and these may be barriers to innovative ideas. However, these constraints may also be seen as opportunities for a social entrepreneur who is able to frame an issue or problem in a new way and present a novel and feasible solution or venture idea. As described in Chapter 3, in order to build an understanding of the public policy element of the community ecosystem, social entrepreneurs cannot ignore the existence of policy fields. And his or her venture may have the potential to re-shape the policy field. Especially in rapidly changing environments or even crisis situations with a lot of uncertainty, individuals can and do challenge the existing institutional order using social skills to create entirely new fields or transform existing ones.[5] In public policy processes, these people are sometimes referred to as "policy entrepreneurs" who look for opportunities to link existing solutions and problems when the political environment is ripe to move an issue onto the public's agenda for change.[6] A social entrepreneur has a similar opportunity once he or she more thoroughly understands the policy arena, the flows of resources and authority, relationships among institutional players, networks of local actors, and the relative power of these players and actors. This kind of understanding is often critical to the success of socially entrepreneurial venture.

Below are five steps that form the basis for a policy field analysis along with specific tools to help complete the steps.

Step 1. Identify the Particular Substantive Policy Issue and Its Policy Domain

Policy field analysis, similar to early stages in the social entrepreneurship process, begins with identifying the particular issue, such as inadequate access to healthy food for an impoverished neighborhood, and then identifying the policy domain of the issue. A policy domain describes the general, substantive issue (such as access to healthy food) and the set of actors, political systems, and institutions most involved in that issue. Within each policy domain there is technical knowledge about the problem and often shared beliefs regarding viable solutions[7] Depending on the issue, it may be more or less easy to identify a single policy domain.[8] For example, "inadequate access to healthy food for an impoverished neighborhood" could fall under the policy domains of poverty, food and food access, and even community and economic development.

For a social entrepreneur, how the venture issue is framed (what is the key problem to be addressed?) will establish a primary policy domain and also suggest what other policy areas may be affected. In Chapter 2 we discussed the initial thinking needed about the issue for the venture, and this chapter builds on that thinking. Defining the problem domain or arena is also an opportunity for the social entrepreneur—he or she may find that how he has framed the issue (the problem definition) and/or the ideas (the solutions) actually crosses well-established policy domains, creating a novel way of understanding and approaching a problem and its solution. For example, while the federal Head Start program was initially framed in terms of employment policy, it has since also been described as crucial to early childhood education and poverty reduction policy domains.

Step 2. Brainstorm List of Actors, Organizations, and Institutions Involved

As we discussed in Chapter 3 through the community ecology framework, most locales (communities) have a limited number of institutions engaged in work that directly bears on the issue. The social entrepreneur can take the results from the community ecology framework and expand from there by brainstorming a more complete list of organizations, considering both those with formal public authority (such as legislative bodies, federal, state, and local government agencies and departments) and those with formal and/or informal relationships to the issue (such as nonprofit service providers, advocacy organizations, professional associations, intermediaries, evaluators, and academic institutions) who have some important involvement in the policy domain.

Table 4.1. Sample Stakeholder Analysis

Stakeholder	What is their interest or stake in issue	What is their activity in the issue area
Institutions (government agencies)		
Community organizations		
Other informal groups, coalitions, etc.		
Funders		
Key individuals		

Essentially, this step involves using the work from the community ecosystem modeling to create a modified stakeholder analysis where the social entrepreneur lists all those individuals, formal and informal groups, organizations, and institutions that have a stake in the policy domain or domains as defined by the venture. Next to each stakeholder, the social entrepreneur can describe what "stake" or interest the stakeholder has in the policy domain and, specifically, what programs or services the stakeholder is providing. For example, is the stakeholder primarily a funder? A service provider? A well-established group of concerned community members? Table 4.1 shows a sample stakeholder sheet.

For social entrepreneurs already active in a particular arena, such brainstorming may be easy because it uses knowledge they have developed through their work. For those entering a new field, social entrepreneurs may need to do some background research and meet with leaders in the field in order to gain a more complete understanding of who is involved, what their interests in the issue are, and what specific activities, programs, services, and so forth they may already be providing that relate to the social entrepreneur's venture issue and idea.

Step 3. Understand Laws and Regulations, Administrative Authority, and Public Funding Streams

Following Step 2 with the stakeholder list assembled, policy field analysis then turns to understanding the structure of the field. The "structure of the field" refers to the institutional mandates and existing resource flows that are central to work on a public issue. The structure of the policy field is what often differentiates work that addresses public problems from work in private industry. In essence, in this part of the analysis, the social entrepreneur is gathering information on the nature of public investment in solving the problem and determining where administrative authority lays. Administrative authority entails the formal power, usually granted by Congress or state legislatures to a government agency, to address the problem and may include program requirements, regulations, and various types of funding resources. This part of the analysis is really focusing on formal authority systems that exist within a policy domain and have the potential to significantly impact the venture issue. These formal authority systems often include sets of "vertical" roles and relationships among, for example, federal agencies that have Congressional mandates and authority to implement programs through specific state agencies and/or local governmental entities. Funding may parallel these mandates where state agencies or local governments receive federal monies to implement specific programs. State and local government may then use these funds to contract with a variety of community organizations or other government entities, for the actual delivery of the programs to targeted beneficiaries. The flows of mandates, administrative authority, and funding can be complex and confusing, especially to the social entrepreneur who is new to a policy area. However, understanding how this field works is critical to his or her ability to operate knowledgably, recognize barriers and seize opportunities.

More specifically, the social entrepreneur needs to pay attention to three particular aspects of field structure.

1. First, the social entrepreneur must understand relevant laws and regulations that bear on his or her venture and exist within the policy domain. Often legislative and regulatory systems establish the boundaries of a policy domain and even how the problem has been defined at the federal, state, or local levels. Legislation and regulations set parameters around what the issue is, what public goals are, and/or who is responsible for meeting those goals.

2. Second, the social entrepreneur needs to determine where administrative authority lies—put simply, who is primarily responsible for implementing legislative goals or regulations? Does this authority lie

at the federal, state, or local level? While a social entrepreneur may concentrate his or her efforts at a very local level and recognize that the city or county has a real interest in the venture's issue, the state or federal government may actually hold the critical authority when it comes to meeting legal mandates and regulations, or making funding decisions.

3. Third, the social entrepreneur needs to be clear how public funding flows and what strings may be attached to this funding. Through which kind of policy instrument or tool will the particular government agency act? Increasingly, governments use a variety of tools, including grants, contracts, loans and loan guarantees, and vouchers. Each tool comes with its own set of assumptions, rules, licensing standards, and requirements.[9] In the early childhood education example above, we see government at different levels using grants (federal to nonprofit), contracts (county to nonprofit), and voucher-like subsidies (state to county to nonprofit).

Step 3 is often illuminating and critically important because it reveals barriers to entry as well as opportunities. Are mandates and funding flows concentrated within a single government agency in the federal government? If so, this may present a barrier or constraint on your idea because the agency has well-entrenched rules and relationships for dealing with its definition of the problem and it may have a federal or national view of the problem, rather than a more particular local sensibility. On the other hand, are these authority and funding flows splintered among several government agencies, as in the case of early childhood education? Fragmentation can create an opportunity for a venture to integrate at the local level if enough support can be garnered to solve a problem differently than in the past.

Through a systematic identification of major public policies, the configuration of their funds and administrative mechanisms, the social entrepreneur-as-analyst comes to understand the forces structuring the particular field. To better represent the interplay between institutional actors and public policies, it is often useful to begin to create a *visual representation of the field*.[10] When full developed, these word-and-arrow diagrams help to trace influence and resource flows.

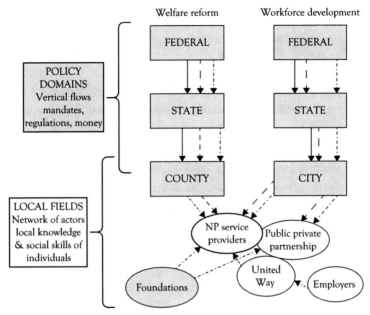

Figure 4.1. Example of a policy field.

As illustrated in Figure 4.1, the first step in this mapping is to summarize the information from the questions above to highlight the flow of: (a) administrative authority for implementation; (b) legislative and regulatory mandates; and, (c) funding flows. Step 4 below will add more local knowledge to this map but as a first step, the social entrepreneur develops the broad contours of the structure of policy field. These maps can become quite complex but it is important to understand that the process of creating these maps through asking and answering a series of focused questions is what really comprises the analysis. In this particular map, the primary issue concerns the social welfare policy domain, for example, improving the lives of single mothers in poverty. A secondary but related policy domain, depending on the venture's focus, may be the workforce development policy domain because of its influence over helping these women prepare for and find jobs. All three levels of government are involved in this issue (federal, state, and local, including both county and city governments) but in different ways. It is up to the social entrepreneur to discover what kinds of relationships exist among these institutional actors.

Step 4. Within the State and Local Context, Determine What Organizations and Groups Have Interest in and Influence Over This Problem

The fourth step in policy field analysis focuses on gaining a deeper understanding of relationships, especially in the local context. In this step, both the stakeholder analysis from Step 2 and the visual map from Step 3 are important tools.

Certainly, many different types of relationships exist within policy fields. So far in our analysis, we have asked questions about formal authority (legal and regulatory) and funding relationships, primarily among government institutional players. Now it is time to expand those relationships to include the local, nongovernmental players as well as additional types of relationships concerning politics, service or product delivery, and problem expertise. In other words, while we concentrated on vertical relationships of formal authority, we are now going to concentrate more on horizontal relationships where both formal and, importantly, informal authority reside. A lot of the information collected from the community ecology analysis in Chapter 3 is central to this piece of the policy field analysis.

Start on the map by drawing different types or colors of lines which represent major flows of authority and funding. Funding flows may now include, for example, local foundations that have a history of giving grants or other resources to your problem area. Some new authority relationships may also emerge at this stage—for example, you may find that a local government agency has given some program design and funding authority to a formal coalition of service providers. Figure 4.1 shows some potentially important actors at the local level in the example above concerning a venture that wants to focus on single women living in poverty.

Political relationships may be difficult to discern but through a few interviews with key informants in the field, the social entrepreneur can ask questions about who or which organizations and people seem most central in the policy arena and have the power to influence key policies and programs. There may be city council members, county commissioners, state legislators, longstanding citizen advocates or community activists that share a similar passion about your issue and have a history of trying to frame how the issue should be defined and/or solved.

Service or product delivery relationships concern understanding who may be "producing" similar programs (see the section on "Substitute Products" in Chapter 5 and how they get the service or product to the end beneficiary). These relationships may simply represent client referral patterns, government contractual relationships, or they may be more complicated, especially if a collaboration is involved in program delivery.

Issue expertise and information are essential to understanding the informal structure of a field.[11] This knowledge is more often tacit than it is explicit, so it can be difficult to acquire if the social entrepreneur is new to the field. However, the social entrepreneur can gradually build this piece of the analysis as she interviews key local players and begins to build her own network of resources and relationships. Likely this expertise resides within some of the individuals identified as having political influence or a long history of program delivery.

The use of social network analysis can help sharpen this part of the overall policy analysis through the kinds of questions it asks:[12]

- Which organizations are more or less central in the policy field? Centrality in a network is often associated with power because of the ability of a centrally positioned organization to control flows of resource such as funding, information, and legitimacy.
- What kinds of ties between and among members are most important? Common types of ties include client referrals, funding, and formal contractual ties.
- Which network members have ties outside of the network that could be used to build support or gather new ideas for the venture?

Even if the social entrepreneur does not conduct a formal social network analysis, asking these questions and summarizing them on a visual map can greatly enhance the ability of the social entrepreneur to understand the contours of the policy field.

Finally, in this step, the social entrepreneur needs to return to his/her stakeholder analysis from Step 2 and revise it to include (or remove) stakeholders uncovered since its creation.

Step 5. Summarize Results of Policy Field Analysis

It is now important for the social entrepreneur to step back and reflect on the results of his or her analysis so far. First, where does he or she need to collect more information? Is this information technical in nature, for example, gaining a deeper understanding of aspects of the issue itself or the specific laws and regulations that bear on issue? Or, is the information more about the relationships and networks at the local level that seem vitally important to understanding the contours of the venture issue? Second, where do there seem to be real and concrete constraints in this policy field? Are there legal or regulatory constraints that would be very difficult to overcome or are constraints more because people and organizations have defined an approach to the venture issue that differs from the way in which the social entrepreneur is framing the issue? In other words, what realistic assessment can the social entrepreneur make about the constraints that have surfaced in the analysis? Third, what gaps seems to exist, especially at the local level, for addressing the venture issue? This is often just the reverse of a constraint identified above—if most organizations are approaching the issue in one way, there may be an opportunity to develop a venture that re-frames the issues and provides a new way of thinking about programs or services. Table 4.2 provides a sample sheet for how to organize some of these summary thoughts.

Table 4.2. Summary Policy Field Analysis

	Describe Opportunity	Describe Constraints	Ideas for Overcoming Constraints
Policy domain			
Laws or regulations			
Administrative authority			
Funding			
Local networks			

Summary

This chapter has focused the social entrepreneur on the policy environment that is most relevant to his or her venture concept. Because most social entrepreneurial ventures exist to solve an important public problem or issue, the social entrepreneur needs to understand several facets of the public policy context that bear on the problem. A policy fields analysis allows the social entrepreneur to systematically work through several sets of questions in order to determine:

1. The issue or problem's primary policy domain.
2. All the relevant stakeholders at the local, state, and national levels who have interests and influence over the problem.
3. Legislative and regulatory mandates that currently exist concerning how the problem is to be addressed and by whom
   a. Administrative authority for carrying out those mandates
   b. Funding flows.
4. Local networks of influential organizations, individuals, and institutions.

The result of a policy field analysis is a better understanding not only of the context surrounding the venture but also of significant constraints and potential opportunities.

Venture Development Questions

1. What policy domain does your venture issue address? Are there other important policy domains that impact your issue?
2. What specific organizations, institutions, and other formal or informal groups are involved? How?
3. What are relevant institutional mandates and regulations affecting this policy domain? Where does administrative authority lay? What types of funding exists and through what mechanisms (for example, through contracts, grants, fees-for-service, etc.).

4. Who is involved at the local level? How? What are the important relationships among these local actors? Who has been centrally involved in the issue?
5. Are there important allies or collaborators at the local level?
6. Overall, what are the critical barriers for your venture concept? Where are opportunities?

CHAPTER 5

Analyzing Competitive Forces—The Market and the Industry

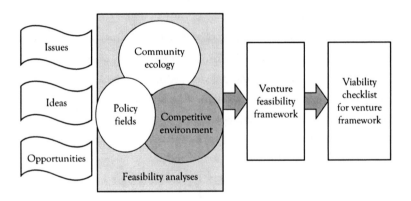

"*The world of competitive market dynamics presents difficult paradoxes to many who work in the NGO sector. They believe that their organization's strength, fueled by the staff's primary motivation, is in its determination to help people improve their lives. But in this more competitive NGO world, it is no longer enough to simply have good intentions and a strong value orientation.*"

Lindenberg (2001)

Learning Goals

1. Understand how competitive analysis in the social sector's environment is similar and different from a business's competitive environment.
2. Understand and apply a social entrepreneurial version of Porter's classic competitive analysis tool.

Determining Critical Competitive Forces

Porter's classic competitive analysis of industries[1] is a useful framework to include in a social entrepreneur's toolbox. Modifications of this framework have been applied in the nonprofit setting with mixed results because some do not believe that a "competitive" view is aligned with their visions and missions. While we appreciate this perspective, we disagree (see, for example, the quotation at the beginning of this chapter, taken from Marc Lindenberg).[2] Some for-profit inspired thinking and analysis are especially useful for social entrepreneurs because this thinking and analysis ask critical questions about a venture concept's viability and ultimately its feasibility.

Here, we use Porter's competitive analysis framework primarily to help the social entrepreneur think more systematically about the community institutions and organizations detailed in Chapters 3 and 4. In particular, our approach to Porter's framework is to use it *in combination* with the community ecology framework and policy fields analysis to provide a thorough understanding on the part of the social entrepreneur of the context in which his or her venture is embedded.

More specifically, there are several reasons why a modified competitive analysis is especially useful during the early stages of a social venture idea's development. First, much like a marketplace-focused venture would study the industry, the social entrepreneur needs to determine whether competitive or complementary programs already exist and to assess their competency and capacity. This analysis can determine whether the venture idea is too duplicative of what exists or, instead, fills a unique niche. Second, the analysis can also begin to identify potential, supporting partners who fit into the substitute products, buyer or seller categories. Third, the analysis pushes the social entrepreneur to think more deeply about resource suppliers, and, importantly, target markets, customers, and demand, something often foreign to those in the nonprofit sector.[1,4]

As with any of the analytical frameworks presented so far, it is easy to get "stuck" trying to do a thorough industry analysis, and, Porter in fact does emphasize thoroughness and deep analysis. Our focus, on the other hand, is on the series of questions raised by the Five Forces Framework to help the social entrepreneur see his or her venture from a broader perspective that includes key elements of the external environment and systematically address each of the elements, deciding for himself which of these elements is most relevant to his venture idea.

Applying Porter's Analysis in a Social Entrepreneurship Environment

Among the underlying assumptions of competitive analysis, three are especially relevant to the social entrepreneur. The first is that she needs at this point to focus in on the economic structure of her venture's "industry" after having targeted cultural and social structures in Chapter 3 and policy and political structures in Chapter 4. Second, Porter defines industries as a collection of firms that produce products that are close substitutes for each other. For a social entrepreneur, industry can be better understood as the (usually) local field or network of formal and informal groups working on the venture issue and similar problems. Third, Porter's focus is on competitive forces and usefully pushes the social entrepreneur to view competitors beyond well-established players. For social entrepreneurs, we focus the analysis not only on competitive forces but also on identification of potential collaborators who may be important allies in any systems change effort.[5] Below are brief descriptions of the five forces and our translation to the social entrepreneurship context.

Figure 5.1. Porter's five forces.

Threat of New Entrants/Barriers to Entry

This part of the analysis focuses on whether coming into this industry will be relatively easy or difficult and includes assessing indicators like economies of scale, customer loyalty, well-established distribution channels, and government policies and regulation. These are all easily translatable to the social entrepreneurship context.

Economies of scale refer to declines in cost per unit that occur when producing larger volumes of these units because fixed costs are spread out over more units. This is a barrier to entry because it means that a new firm will have to come in at a larger scale than is often feasible. In our context, it means the social entrepreneur needs to understand whether he or she needs to provide a large volume of the service or activity in order to capture economies that existing players have already realized. Porter also discusses how experience in an industry can lead to cost declines. This is relevant in our context—does the social entrepreneur and/or his team possess a unique set of knowledge and experiences that will be difficult to replicate by others? For example, a social entrepreneur wants to establish a restaurant run by clients from a homeless shelter. He has a long career in the restaurant business and has well-established networks in the local areas. Those experiences and networks are critical to the success of any new restaurant business and are very difficult to replicate. These experiences are an opportunity he can exploit when moving forward to design his venture. The experiences also may reduce his costs in terms of time spent cultivating relationships or money spent in hiring a consultant to advise him on the restaurant business.

If a venture depends on getting referrals of clients, then a question is whether there are already well-established referral patterns (distribution channels) that will be difficult to change. A government agency may have longstanding contracts with certain nonprofit provider organizations that will be very difficult to disrupt or alter by a new socially entrepreneurial venture. For example, workforce development programs offered by nonprofits may have established contracts with local city agencies that could be difficult to dislodge even if the social entrepreneur is convinced that he or she has a better idea of how to get hard-to-employ people back to work.

Are clients or beneficiaries already loyal to existing programs? Some ventures, for example, in child care, may depend on reputation and trust and close relationships between those served and those providing the service. In fact, according to one nonprofit expert, reputation is the major barrier to entry in most nonprofit markets.[6] In this situation, convincing beneficiaries to change programs (or "brands") may be difficult. On the other hand, if established programs do not have an especially good reputation or have recently come under fire in the media, this may provide an opportunity to offer something new and reputable.

Government policies and regulations are also a part of the assessment of barriers to entry, and these have been addressed more thoroughly in Chapter 4. For our purposes here, the social entrepreneur can use his or her overall assessment of the constraints and opportunities from the policy field analysis to note whether existing policies, legal mandates, and regulations provide significant barriers to entry.

Threat of Substitute Products

This category emphasizes the need to understand first, what are relevant substitute products, and second, among these substitutes, what important price-performance trade-offs exist. To think about substitute products, Porter emphasizes analyzing products that perform similar functions for consumers. The price-performance trade-off refers to the relationship between price and performance (for example, a high price with an expectation that performance will likewise be of high quality). A new venture that offers an alternative to that established trade-off may find it difficult to enter the marker.

In our context, we encourage the social entrepreneur to think not only about obviously similar programs, services, or products but also those that may be becoming similar in eyes of clients or beneficiaries. Who else is doing something similar to the new venture idea? For example, a program to offer public bicycles at specified locations in a city's downtown may find that potential consumers see this program as a substitute for low-cost, short-term car rentals offered at similar locations. Finding out that others are doing related work is not a reason to stop developing the idea. Rather, it is important to push on whether and how the venture is unique and fulfills an important niche. It may also guide the social entrepreneur to refine their target population to better distinguish themselves from others.

Additionally, as mentioned earlier, asking the question about substitute products can help the social entrepreneur identify potential collaborators and partners. For example, in the bicycle rental venture, the social entrepreneur might find that the short-term car rental entrepreneurs would be good partners in a joint marketing campaign to reduce urban traffic congestion. This kind of joint marketing might be quite attractive to potential funders.

The Bargaining Power of Suppliers and of Buyers[7]

Assessing the power of suppliers and buyers begins to address questions of resources for the venture as well as the demand potential of the target population. Power in this context relates to the degree of dependency between organizations. Do suppliers have many or few organizations that need their resources? If suppliers have many organizations they can supply, then supplier power is relatively high. If suppliers only have a few organizations that need their resource, then supplier power is low. Likewise for buyers—if buyers can choose among many organizations for a particular product, then buyer power is high relative to those organizations. If, on the other hand, buyers have limited options, then buyer power is low.

Suppliers in the social entrepreneur's realm primarily include resource suppliers such as funders, sources of referrals of clients and the supply of labor (paid and unpaid). Especially with regard to funders, questions need to be asked about whether there are several or only a few appropriate funders and how well-established are their funding relationships with grantees or contractors? In other words, are funders concentrated (there are only a few potential funders) and do they have a lot of choices (many grantees chasing after their dollars) when it comes to their funding decisions? If the answers to both questions are "yes," then their power is high, and it may be less likely they will take a chance on a new venture. The power of labor markets can also be important for some ventures. For example, if the venture depends on volunteer labor for its operation, is this labor pool relatively large and "unattached," or does the venture need a special kind of volunteer? Do these volunteers already have many other choices of volunteer opportunities?

For example, a new venture proposed to use volunteers from a small group of local churches to launch a matching service with low-income elderly who needed a variety of home maintenance and personal services. While the churches were willing to entertain the venture idea, most of them already provided volunteers from their congregations for existing projects.

Buyers are primarily the customers for the market driven venture project. For many social entrepreneurial ventures the buyer can be the one served. Importantly, the central social venture customer may not be the people served by the venture and this is often the case. For example, in Twin Cities RISE!, an organization dedicated to alleviating concentrated poverty through long-term employment of the hard-to-employ, the primary customers are the employers who hire the hard-to-employ.[8] For a social entrepreneur who has studied their target population and community as described in Chapter 3, the question should be answered using that understanding of who will be served and who will be "buying" the service. Again, similar to suppliers, questions concern whether buyers are concentrated (there are only a few of them) and whether they can "buy" a similar program, product, or service from many others? Will the venture provide something unique *from their perspective*? Answering this question depends on the social entrepreneur's having done some analysis of the question of "substitute products," since he or she needs to determine what options may exist from the buyer's point of view.

Intensity of Rivalry in the Industry

The final category in a social entrepreneur's competitive analysis concerns his or her assessment of the overall intensity of rivalry in this industry. One can use the stakeholder analysis from Chapter 4 to get a basic sense of the number, size, and characteristics of others who are operating within the venture's field. A few big players suggest a stable industry that may be difficult to penetrate. These large organizations may have established the "rules of the game," in Porter's terms, which reduce opportunities to break into the industry. In our context, we may examine this aspect of Porter as a question of "turf." In some cases, existing agencies may have come to some implicit or explicit understanding about who does what within the problem area. For example, the social entrepreneur may have determined that there are longstanding collaborative relationships among a few large, well-established social welfare nonprofits who either formally or informally have established a boundary around a problem domain that is difficult to penetrate. They might have each invested a lot of human and physical assets in developing programs and therefore have a high stake in maintaining the status quo. They may also have established long-term funding or contractual relationships with, for example, government funders, who also have a stake in maintaining these relationships and erecting barriers to entry.[9] Even if the social entrepreneur concludes that the industry is relatively stable, he or she may also find that it is an opportune time to insert change. In this case, however, the social entrepreneur must be prepared for a push back ("we have always done it that way") that may limit his opportunity to enter the field.

On the other hand, many diverse competitors suggest instability and more opportunities for entry. Diversity here means that organizations in a problem area are using a number of different strategies and that these are diverse in terms of their overall aims, values, and approaches to problem-solving. For the social entrepreneur, instability may be fertile ground for innovation and entry but understanding the politics of this instability will be essential. For example, a new venture focused on getting men committed to helping solve the problem of human trafficking found that the domestic abuse field was fragmented and ideologically split among several key groups. While the venture had to learn the politics of the field, it found an opportunity to develop a niche for its programs while also initiating collaborations among heretofore competitors.

Summary

This chapter argues that a modified competitive analysis is useful to the social entrepreneur, especially in combination with the community ecology and policy fields frameworks, because it sharpens the social entrepreneur's attention to competitive or complementary programs that already exist, helps the social entrepreneur identify potential supporters and collaborators (not just competitors), and deepens the ability of the social entrepreneur to

Table 5.1. Porter's Five Forces Applied to Social Entrepreneurship Context

	Market-oriented application	Social entrepreneurship application
Threat of new market entrants	How easy or difficult is it to break into this industry?	Are there established relationships, mandates, or funding flows that create important barriers?
Threat of substitute products (including technology change)	What is the price-performance trade-off among products that can be substituted?	What other formal or informal entities are providing similar programs, products or services?
Bargaining power of suppliers	How concentrated or dispersed are suppliers? Do they have many or a few firms to choose among?	Are there only a few potential funders for your venture? Do they have many choices of entities to fund? How about paid or unpaid labor markets?
Bargaining power of buyers	How concentrated or dispersed are buyers? Are there just a few buyers who have a lot of similar choice or are there many buyers with few choices?	Are there only a few buyers in your target market or many? Do they have many choices or only a few from which to "purchase?"
Existing competitive rivalry	Have a few firms established a stable understanding of the rules of the game? Or, are many diverse competitors swirling around the industry with different approaches and strategies?	What "turf" issues exist in your venture's problem area? Is there a set of well-established programs who have "agreed" upon who does what or are there many programs competing for the same turf?

understand the positions and perspectives of resource suppliers and buyers. Table 5.1 summarizes the five forces in Porter's competitive analysis and applies them to the social entrepreneurship context.

Venture Development Questions

1. What are the key barriers to entry in this field? How important are economies of scale, established patterns of relationships, and reputation in this field?

2. What substitute services or programs exist in the field? Does the venture offer something truly unique?

3. Are there many or few potential beneficiaries? Have they already established relationships with existing organizations or groups in the field? How about suppliers of resources, including funders as well as supply of paid staff and volunteers?

4. Overall, how competitive is this field? Are there many groups and organizations or only a few? Are they large and well-established or small and fragmented? What are their relationships among each other?

CHAPTER 6

Creating a Social Venture Feasibility Plan

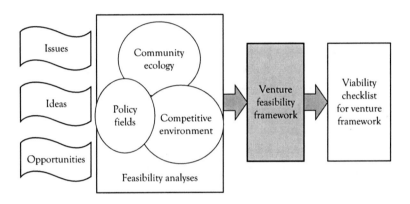

"All endeavor calls for the ability to tramp the last mile, shape the last plan, endure the last hours toil. The fight to the finish spirit is the one... characteristic we must possess if we are to face the future as finishers."

Henry David Thoreau

Learning Goals

1. The social entrepreneur is able to bring together the results of the creativity and analysis described in Chapters 2–5.
2. The social entrepreneur is able to complete a written feasibility plan.

A venture feasibility plan is an integrative narrative that reflects the creative ideas, research, and decisions that have been generated about the intended venture during the analytical processes. The plan is used to determine if the basic framework of the venture is viable and likely to thrive. A social venture feasibility plan pulls together the work the social entrepreneur has been doing as she deepens her understanding of the issue and solutions. A venture feasibility plan goes beyond just summarizing that work, however, because it also narrows down approaches to the problem, begins to detail what kinds of resources the venture will need, and establishes initial outcomes and outcome measures.

This chapter discusses each part of the social venture feasibility plan using the information and analyses gathered in Chapters 3–5. At the end of each of those chapters are questions to guide the social entrepreneur in drawing the conclusions called for in that chapter. This chapter uses those conclusions and weaves them into a framework that is a precursor to the full venture plan and a guide for how to select from among many strategic action options facing the social entrepreneur. The resulting narrative becomes a blueprint draft that then can guide the more intensive work needed to be ready to launch.

Sometimes a section in the venture feasibility plan cannot be fully completed as there are still important unanswered questions. Those questions are also written down and become part of the next steps needed to move to a fully complete venture plan. Once the feasibility plan is complete, the viability of the venture can be assessed for determining the next steps. That will be described in Chapter 7.

The Social Venture Feasibility Plan Outline

The work of creating the venture feasibility plan is done when the social entrepreneur writes down in narrative form the vision, desired result, and set of strategies that will guide his or her work. The venture feasibility plan includes:

1. The vision of success, the change to be created, a discussion of the problem to be addressed, its scale and scope in the target community and its likely causes.
2. A brief description of the proposed product or service.
3. A description of the target population and community to be the focus of the action.
4. A delineation of existing barriers to progress and their extensiveness.

5. A description of assumptions that guide the venture approach.

6. The Working Model description which includes the chosen approaches to the problem and how those approaches will be implemented, backed up by a summary of the relevant evidence that those actions are the right ones.

7. A list of desired short- and long-term outcomes of the venture's work.

8. A discussion of the resources needed including the human, physical and financial resources with a discussion of the likely resource sources.

9. A timeline for start-up and operations for the first 1–2 years.

10. Expected early evidence and measures of progress toward longer term outcomes.

1. Setting a Vision for Success

A vision statement describes the change that the venture hopes to achieve over time. Sometimes called Impact statements, these statements describe a future, 7–10 years out that will result if all the work by the venture is successful. A vision is the ultimate change that the venture hopes to bring about. Often a vision is the ideal that would occur if all the barriers to success were overcome for the population and or community in focus.

A vision statement includes enough information to describe the issue/problem and how it could be changed. It describes the best long-term future possible. It is inspirational for all who are engaged in the venture. Vision statements are different from mission statements. Carter McNamara, a nationally recognized consultant and author on nonprofit management, writes that a mission statement is a concise statement of what the organization does. The vision statement is a "vivid description of the organization as it effectively carries out its operations."[1]

It is the vision statement that is important to draft for a venture framework. The Foundation Center suggests the following question guide this discernment, "What would you ultimately hope to accomplish as a result of your efforts?"[2] However you begin, the resulting statement should be one that inspires commitment and can be used to guide choices faced as operational decisions are made. Here are some examples of vision statements for existing organizations:

- Ensuring every child has a successful start in life (Way to Grow, Minneapolis, Minnesota).
- A growing movement of leaders, now 33,000 strong, works at every level of education, policy and other professions, to ensure that all children can receive an excellent education (Teach for America).[3]
- Every person has the opportunity to achieve his/her fullest potential and participate in and contribute to all aspects of life (Good Will Industries International, Inc.).[4]
- Our vision is to leave a sustainable world for future generations (Nature Conservancy).[5]

2. Describing the Problem and Its Possible Causes

Chapter 2 describes the issue or problem scanning process, and Chapters 3–5 also contribute to understanding the issue with deeper analyses. The result of these analyses grounds the venture and reinforces a specific focus for action. Human issues are complicated and often intertwined. An effective venture focuses on an issue, working to reduce that problem and its consequences. The clearer the issue focus is, the more likely it is that the actions selected will be effective. Clarity of understanding of the selected issue is necessary in order to more readily determine the change desired.

For this part of the social venture feasibility plan, it is important to include enough detail to set the groundwork for the venture itself. A good problem description provides the rationale for the actions selected and defines the perspective on the issue by the venture. That detail also helps anyone else engaged in the venture to understand the issue. The issue summary should include answers to the following questions, many of which the social entrepreneur started to answer in Chapter 2:

a. What are the key current facts about the issue? What is the extent of the problem or issue? How long has it been around?
b. What are the consequences if the problem is not addressed?
c. What are known or suspected causes for the issue or problem?
d. What has been tried in the past to address the issue?

3. Describing the Product or Service

A description of what the product or service is added next. What will be offered? What makes it unique? Where will it be located? What will the customer or client experience? Remember that most of the time the reader of this plan will not be familiar with the service or product field; therefore include a description of the attributes of the product or service. This section is actually best completed after drafting section 7, the working model, as it is a summary of what is determined from the working model development.

4. Describing the Target Population and Target Community

Creating this section of a social venture feasibility plan starts with the answers the drafted for the questions at the end of Chapter 3. The target population is a group of people that are the intended beneficiaries of the social entrepreneurial venture. A target population is described by what the people have in common. It can be described by demographic characteristics, common behaviors, common problems, illnesses, geographic area of residence, etc. Target populations can also be selected for their common psychographics such as attitudes, lifestyle choices, or living conditions.

Some ventures have more than one target population and then select a set of distinct action strategies to respond to these differences. Some ventures have primary target populations and secondary ones. For example, a program aimed to improve academic achievement of elementary school-aged children will often have a secondary target population that includes the parents of those children or those who teach them.

When writing this section of the social venture feasibility plan, it is important to ensure the following questions are answered with enough factual detail to allow the scale and scope of the venture's reach to be understood.

1. What are the characteristics of the population to be reached?
2. Using specific facts what is the size of the target population: What are the key common attributes, including, for example:
   ○ socio-demographic: age, sex, family, size, income, occupation, social class, etc.

- ○ geography: national, regional, urban/rural, density,
- ○ psychographics: lifestyle, personality, attitudes, cultural practices
- ○ behaviors: benefits being sought, purchasing rate, usage rate, etc.

3. How has the issue affected their lives?

Sample target population description:

Twin Cities RISE! The Population We Serve

- ○ *The Core Program served 624 low-income adults living in the Twin Cities in 2012*
- ○ *Under employed and unemployed adults*
- ○ *Hardest to serve adults, typically with extensive barriers such as generational poverty, criminal histories, chemical dependency, mental health issues, homelessness, and chronic unemployment*
- ○ *Predominately African–American men, though program open to all*
- ○ *Must have less than $7,000 in assets upon entering program[6]*

5. Assessing Barriers to Progress

Effectively addressing an issue or problem requires an understanding of the barriers to progress that have blocked success on addressing an issue. This understanding requires a review of the issue, the target community, the policy fields surrounding the issue and the actions of others in the industry. These analyses were all discussed in Chapters 3–5. Now it is time to synthesize what you have learned about why the issue still persists.

Barriers to progress can be found in resistance to change that can often be seen as "old habits" and common practices that reinforce negative behaviors or block progress. The resistance comes from many fronts: individual behaviors, peer group behaviors, family behaviors and structures, cultural practices, community structures, political structures and policies and the physical environment as well. Understanding all of these aspects of an issue increases the likelihood that an approach to the problem will be successful. The previous chapters have been guides on how to do the analysis of these factors that reinforce the status quo and create barriers to change. The chapters have also shown the possible entry points for change, resources available, and likely allies.

Understanding the reasons people have for resisting change will add to the understanding necessary to select the best set of approaches. Rosabeth Moss Kanter lists the following possibilities in a September 2012 blog for Harvard Business Review: fear of loss of control, high degree of uncertainty about the future, loss of face, concern about competency to do what is called for, past negative experiences.[7]

Sometimes this list of barriers becomes overwhelming. A simple listing does not provide guidance on where to start or show the best points of entry into the problem that will cause a cascading of positive impact on the issue. Just deepening the search for relevant facts is not enough. So a process is needed to sift through all the information. Where to start? Often the social issue in focus is one that has many symptoms. This diversity of symptoms can confound the synthesis work and can make it difficult to understand where the best entry point for action is. Finding the right trigger or triggers that will cause a domino effect of change is important. Without that search, actions can become responses to symptoms that only cover up the underlying cause(s) or barriers that need to be addressed. To aid that search, the social entrepreneur can think about answers to the following questions:

a. What is getting in the way? For each barrier, determine the size and scope and how it blocks progress. Some determination of the persistence and prevalence of the barrier is also important.
b. Who else is working to address that specific barrier?
c. What are the most critical barriers to change, or preconditions for success that must be in place for change to occur?
d. What are the best places to begin the change process? (Note: This answer may best be found in studying the community ecosystem developed in Chapter 3. If, for example, there is a negative public attitude about the issue the first steps may need to focus on changing public opinion.)

6. Describe Assumptions That Guide the Venture Approach

Assumptions may or may not be fact based. They are presuppositions, often beliefs that are taken for granted, but often not proven. Assumptions can be found, for example, in the selection of barriers and in the description of the target population and community. Too often assumptions come only from the limited experience of the entrepreneur himself. They can also come from conversations with those living in the community. They can become clearer during conversations with professionals in the field. While the instincts of those familiar with the community may be tremendously helpful in determining the barriers that are important to remove or overcome, those same instincts are also where false assumptions can be hidden.

American novelist Daniel Handler, under the pen name Lemony Snicket, wrote about the riskiness of assumptions in <u>The Austere Academy</u>.

> "*Assumptions are dangerous things to make, and like all dangerous things to make—bombs, for instance, or strawberry shortcake—if you make even the tiniest mistake you can find yourself in terrible trouble. Making assumptions simply means believing things are a certain way with little or no evidence that shows you are correct, and you can see at once how this can lead to terrible trouble. For instance, one morning you might wake up and make the assumption that your bed was in the same place that it always was, even though you would have no real evidence that this was so. But when you got out of your bed, you might discover that it had floated out to sea, and now you would be in terrible trouble all because of the incorrect assumption that you'd made. You can see that it is better not to make too many assumptions, particularly in the morning.*"[8]

Assumptions should be stated, written down. And once stated, attempts should be made to determine if they are factual. Assumptions can be a range of things such as: accepted cause and effect relationships, level of competency in the target population, availability of resources or complementary services, etc. When the information is analyzed all together, assumptions about what is happening and its causes can be found underlying the lists. A social entrepreneur will be more successful if he takes time to discover and clarify his own assumptions as well as those of others.

Writing assumptions down in the venture drafting process is important. That allows for those assumptions to be checked against the facts, tested for prejudices and inappropriate imposition of the culture of the entrepreneur onto the community in focus. While there will be many written assumptions, the critical ones are those that are tied to the assumed impact resulting from the selected approaches. Acknowledging the assumptions about the long-term effect on the issue in focus are crucial at this stage of plan formation.

> ***Assumptions in planning: (Assumptions are)*** *statements about how and why we expect a set of outcomes to come about as depicted in the (planned) pathway of change. These statements can reflect understandings of the change process taken from research, or they can be taken from practical experience. They should also reflect an understanding of the context within which a program operates. Often assumptions raise questions about the extent to which we can bring about the change we expect, given what we have to work with."*
>
> Andrea A. Anderson
> *The Community Builders Approach to Theory of Change*[9]

The key assumptions should be described in summary along with the possible related facts or areas of inquiry. It is often necessary at this stage to identify areas of needed further research. An assumption should also have linked to it a listing of the decisions that have been made based on that assumption. As further venture development occurs and further information is gathered, those assumptions should be revisited regularly. False assumptions and their related decisions can send a venture down a wrong path. Correcting that path is crucial to success.

For example,

a. Teach For America assumes: filling high-need classrooms with passionate, high-achieving individuals who will do whatever it takes to help their students succeed is a critical piece of our approach—but it's not enough to close the achievement gap. Success relies on the work corps members do as alumni after their two-year commitment, from within the field of education and other sectors, to continue to expand opportunities for all students.[10]

b. Family Assets for Independence in Minnesota assumes: that giving people skills to develop financial assets will be a pathway out of poverty.[11]

7. *The Working Model: Selecting Approaches, Strategies, and Related Operating Structures*

Choosing a primary set of actions to be taken by the venture is a core part of venture planning. "Let's do something and let the chips fall where they may" is not an appropriate approach to addressing human conditions. The viability of a venture framework cannot be determined without a description of what will be done in the venture and an explanation of the expected resulting experience by those served. The elements of a working model include information about what products and/or services will be offered and how it will be delivered. The determination of this set of actions are conclusions made by the social entrepreneur's using analyses of target population needs, likely approaches to overcome barriers to progress, analysis of relevant research and a review of the policy and market environments. Out of this analysis emerges an array of needed actions.

That array of possible actions now needs to be distilled down to a final set of strategies. A venture's selected approach is a combined response to the following questions:

a. What is the set of actions, products and/or services to be offered and in what order?
b. How will those actions, products or services be delivered?
c. Is the venture likely to have the expertise, skills, and resources needed to deliver that?
d. What will the client or customer experience?
e. What research and what assumptions guide the choices made for chosen activities?

Looking at research in the field is critical to the selection of the best combination of strategies and approaches. Research studies should be strong guides to use to find proven approaches to address the issue in focus. In depth searches should be undertaken to find the most current and valid research done on the effective strategies. For example, recently a study on reducing obesity identified a few key change efforts that have strong promise.

Obesity remains an ongoing discussion and finding novel ways to sup-port permanent changes in lifestyle are the subject of a study out of Northwestern Medicine published in the Archives of Internal Medi-cine. It found that simply changing one bad habit has a domino effect on others.

According to the study, by simply knocking down your sedentary leisure time, you'll reduce junk food and saturated fats because you're no longer glued to the TV and mindlessly grazing. It's a two-for-one benefit because the behaviors are closely related. The study also found the most effective way to rehab a delinquent lifestyle requires two key behavior changes: cutting time spent in front of a TV or computer screen and eating more fruits and vegetables. With this simplified strat-egy, people are capable of making big lifestyle changes in a short period of time and maintaining them, according to the study.[12]

Choices about whether prevention, intervention, or crisis response strategies also must be made at this time. Prevention strategies focus on stopping the beginning of an issue. Intervention strategies are actions done after a problem is experienced with the intention of stopping or slowing its progress. The obesity example above is an intervention strategy; it approaches a problem after the individual is at great risk. Teaching young people and their parents about health, fitness, and nutrition is a prevention approach, one that is popular today. In some situations, crisis response is necessary first. The required actions focus on ameliorating the conse-quences of a serious problem. In a crisis, selected strategies focus on deal-ing with the immediate consequences of an event, attempting to block the progress of a crisis or attempting to reduce the immediate threat. Crisis response strategies usually lead to or are part of a set of strategies that together reduce the likelihood of crises occurring in the future.

If prevention is the preferred strategy the entrepreneur needs to take extra caution in selecting the approaches to be used. It is in the prevention

Figure 6.1. Response strategy options.

arena that assumptions based on personal experience can lead the entre-preneur to the selection of ineffective approaches. This is because the effects of prevention actions often are evident many years later and the necessary high quality research about the impact is difficult to do, requir-ing following clients and a control group for many years. Prevention impact research may be available in the issue area of focus. If it is available it can be critical to selecting the best approaches.

Evidence that the specific chosen approaches do make a difference is critical to success. For example, funders often require evidence that the investment they will be making in that approach is cost effective. Thus, it is important to summarize that evidence and share it with all engaged in the venture.

The type of organizational legal form is part of the working model description. The last part of determining the working model is to answer the question: What is the type of organizational form of the venture: non profit, for profit or hybrid?

The basic options for organizational structure are either not for profit 501(c)3 or a form of for-profit structure. We will for simplicity focus on these two structure options. There are organizational structures that are combinations of a nonprofit and a for-profit. These are evolving and fre-quently discussed within the social enterprise associations and journals and at this point are best studied by accessing the most current discussions.

This choice of forms is tied to a number of questions best framed by REDF (Roberts Enterprise Development Fund), a San Francisco based organization widely respected for its extensive work in social entrepreneur-ial efforts and assessment of results. The key questions are:

	501(c)3 Nonprofit	For profit structure
Primary focus	Mission	Profit, excess revenue
Use of Excess revenue	Required to re-invest toward mission	Maybe taken by owners
Ultimately responsible	Board of Directors	Owners
Accountable to	Community	Owners and investors
Formation approvals needed	State and Federal Government, IRS	State

Figure 6.2. Comparing nonprofit and for-profit structures.

1. What is the organization's primary mission—a social goal or a profit goal?
2. What are the founders' perspectives skills, and motivations?
3. What is the market for the primary activities?
4. How closely held is the organization? (assuming nonprofit organizations are widely held)[13]

The choice of structure can be determined after considering these questions. The answer to question 3 may first need an assessment of revenue streams as some revenue sources will only provide funds to nonprofit organizations while others will only provide funds to entities with intentions of earning a profit and providing a return to the investor. That is discussed in section 9 of this chapter.

8. Writing Outcomes—Short and Long Term

What exactly are the specific desired long-term outcomes that should result from the work of the venture? An outcome is a statement about the specific changes that are intended by a social venture. An outcome is a statement that the Collins English dictionary defines as "something that follows from an action, dispute, situation, etc.; result; consequence."[14] For a venture the outcome may be the result of many actions. Determining that change is very important to ensure you make the right choices in developing a venture. It has been the experience of Terri Barreiro that it is best for a venture to have more than one and less than six outcomes. Limiting the number of outcomes is important to ensure continued focused actions. Taking the time to make these simple, clear, precise, and measurable allows for easier action choices.

Outcome statements define the changes in people or communities that are expected to result from the program activities. They are statements of expected achievement or desired consequences. Stated outcomes also become the desired effect against which all possible actions are assessed with the question "will the action most likely contribute to the outcomes we are driving for?" They often define how individuals change, but can also define how a community or system will change. Usually a venture will have multiple desired outcomes.

Stating short-term and long-term desired outcomes sets the direction for the venture. For a particular program, the short-term outcomes are more readily evident, while the long-term outcomes are evident only after the program ends.

Short-term outcomes are results you expect to achieve one to three years after a program activity is under way: Short-term outcomes are specific changes in things like attitudes, behaviors, knowledge, skills, status, or level of functioning expected to result from program activities. These usually are expressed at an individual level among program participants. In selecting short-term outcomes consider any "domino effects" that could result from an early change that would lead to larger long-term changes. For example, youth in a mentoring program who receive one-on-one tutoring and encouragement to improve academic performance may attend school more regularly which can lead to better grades, which can ultimately lead to graduating.[15]

Long-term outcomes are results you expect to achieve in four or more years: Long-term outcomes are also specific changes in things like attitudes, behaviors, knowledge, skills, status, or level of functioning expected to result from program activities. These usually build on the progress expected by the short-term outcomes.[16]

Long-term outcomes may also be kinds of organizational, community, or system level changes expected to result from program activities and which might include improved conditions, increased capacity, and/or changes in the policy arena.

Determining changes in individuals: Changes can be cognitive, affective or behavioral—they have learned something, they think or feel differently, and/or they act differently. The changes are ones that can be observed, demonstrated, or reported by the individual.

Determining changes in the community: Community changes can be physical, economic, political, and more. Change is often stated as a change in behaviors of a total community. For example, a community public health program focused on increasing access to health care for children could have an outcome to reduce the percentage of uninsured children in a specific community.

Many guides to outcome creation use the SMART measure for successful statements.[17]

- **Specific**: concrete; who or what is expected to change
- **Measurable**: can see, hear, count, smell it
- **Attainable**: likely to be achieved
- **Results-oriented**: meaningful, valued results
- **Timed**: target date

Examples of good outcomes

a. Families with low incomes participating in the program increase their purchases of locally grown and organic foods within 3 months after this program finishes.
b. People engaged in this positive persona health awareness program for more than a month report they have less clinic or emergency room visits and are more optimistic about their full recovery.
c. People living in our town use public transportation more frequently for weekly shopping and entertainment trips.

Strong outcomes include the following:

1. A description of who will change, specific reachable population.
2. A description of what will change.
3. A definition of what will be the extent of the change—often tied to a standard.
4. And how the change will be evidenced. (measurable).
5. Each should be stated in action terms, using an active verb.

Things to avoid when writing outcomes:

1. Don't make them general statements, be as specific as possible.
2. Don't focus on things you cannot effect.
3. Avoid "lofty" language, outcomes should be easy for all staff and clients to understand.
4. Output counts are not outcomes. While it is important for programs to monitor levels of service such as attendance or frequency of participation, these are not descriptions of changes expected from the service.
5. Achievement of Internal operational activities or progress on strategic plans is not outcomes either.
6. A statement of time of by when the change is to happen.

Figure 6.3. Considerations for writing outcomes.

    d. Non-English speaking clients in our clinic understand their diagnosis, the treatment plan and know how to practice the necessary home care.

Harry Hatrey from The Urban Institute has done significant work on identifying frequently used measureable outcomes. A review of the website of Urban Institute's Outcome Indicators Project can assist the social entrepreneur to refine their outcome statements.[18]

9. Determining Necessary Resources and Their Sources

A venture feasibility plan must also include a preliminary discussion of the start-up and operating costs, expected revenue streams, and uses of funds.

It is best to start with determining the costs to operate the working model. Information about costs for specific items in the budget can be obtained from other organizations in the geographic area and industry associations or nonprofit management assistance organizations. Questions that need to be answered include:

    a. How will the venture be staffed? What skills and expertise are required? What are the average annual salaries for those employees?
    b. What the non-human expenditures are needed to create the product or services to be provided? (program costs)
    c. What kind of administration costs, space, and equipment will be needed? (operating costs)
    d. What kind of outreach and education (marketing) will be needed to reach those in need of the services to be offered?
    e. What kinds of government fees, professional licenses, and other legal fees are part of the operation?

Figure 6.4 shows a simple budget format that can be used to frame the basic estimates of the operating costs. Budgets from similar operations can often be easily found with a web search or shared by others running similar programs. Expense costs do vary significantly from industry to industry and service type so research within the field is important to get the right understanding of costs.

Pricing a product or service is a difficult but critical part of the resources framework. The first question to answer is: What does it cost

Revenue	Organization Budget
Foundation grants	150,000
Corporate contributions	100,000
United Way	50,000
Individuals donations	40,000
Fees for services—sliding scale	60,000
Contracts for service	50,000
Annual silent auction	10,000
Interest income	2,000
Total Revenue	**$462,000**
Expenses	
Staff salaries and wages	300,000
Fringe benefits 20%	60,000
Rent and utilities	20,000
Equipment and phones	20,000
Office supplies, printing, etc.	10,000
Travel and meetings	15,000
Legal and accounting services	20,000
Miscellaneous	5,000
Total	**$450,000**
Revenue over Expenses	**$12,000**

Figure 6.4. Sample nonprofit budget.

to create and distribute the product or service? First determine how many units of a product or service can be delivered in a given time frame with the staff and operations planned. Using the budget estimates then a rough cost per unit can be established, by simply dividing the total annual budget by the total number of units of product or service to be provided. Another part of the price setting analysis is answering: what does our competition charge? Business cost analysis processes found in most business planning guides can be found to guide a much deeper determination of these costs but for now this short-hand version can be used as a guide.

Next, estimates of revenue streams are necessary. Revenue can come from a wide range of sources. Basically there are four kinds of revenue: fees or product sales to customers or clients, investments by investors expecting a return, grants or contributions from donors expecting a tax deduction, and government contracts tied to performance. Investments are usually only made in for profit organizations and grants or contributions are only made to IRS approved nonprofit organizations. The other two kinds of revenue sources are available to all structure types.

The first revenue related question is how much the customer or client can pay. Each kind of product or service will have all or just a portion of the costs covered from the client or customer served. And in many cases the customer/client actually pays nothing for the service or product. In other cases the customer or client pays all of the costs. A common practice is to offer a sliding scale of fees that is adjusted based on the income of the individual served. To determine what this customer revenue stream could be requires an analysis of what the potential customer or client is able or willing to pay. Usually this means looking at the economic status of the target population but may also include an assessment of the relative importance of the product or service to the customer. A stop smoking service maybe worth paying its cost for the highly motivated person who wants to stop, but not at all a priority for the person who intends to quit later in their life.

A secondary revenue stream tied to the customer can come from their employer or insurance provider. In a stop smoking program for example, employers and health insurance companies have sometimes paid all of the costs for services to a group of people.

If it is determined at this point that all of the revenue needed can come from the customer or a source paying on their behalf then a for-profit structure is a viable option for an operating structure. If the answer to this question is no, then other revenue sources will be needed to subsidize the service delivery and a nonprofit structure is what should be pursued.

Figure 6.5 shows variations that occur around who is paying the costs of the service and how that influences the organizational structure. It also shows how those revenue patterns change the strength of influence by clients on the service provider.

Other revenue sources are possible in a nonprofit structured organization, including foundation grants, government contracts, individual donations, revenue from events as well as revenue from various kinds of related enterprises, such as a store within a museum.

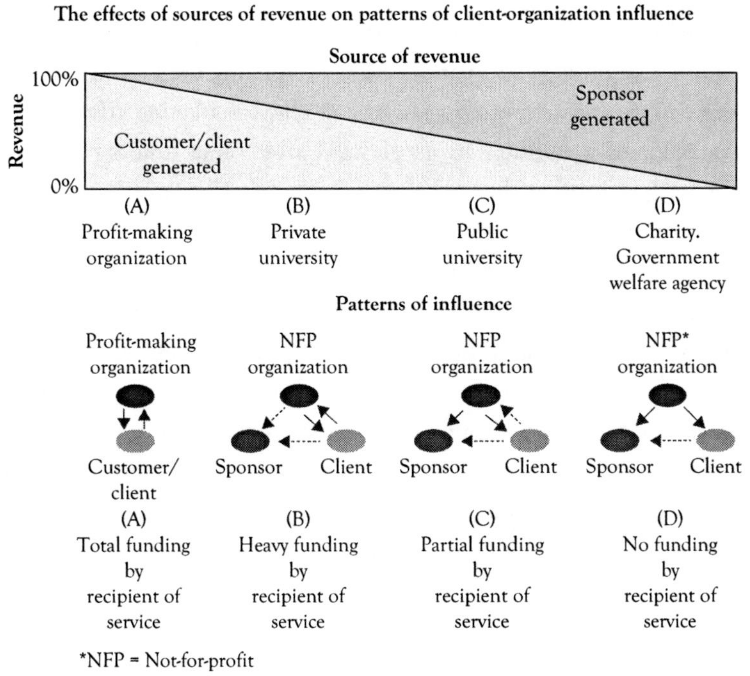

The effects of sources of revenue on patterns of client-organization influence

Figure 6.5. The effects of sources of revenue on patterns of client–organization influence.
Source: Wheelen and Hunger (2006) (reprinted with permission).

Some ventures will also need funds to start the venture. To determine this, one must answer the question: What does it cost to start the venture? Common start-up expenses include equipment, space improvements, office set-up costs, training for new staff, and more. All of these are one time, upfront costs and should be described in the feasibility plan. In a for-profit structure those costs will be covered with funds coming most likely from the founders, family, and friends and in some cases investors. In a nonprofit structure those funds could be obtained through voluntary contributions and grants.

10. Timeline

This section of the social venture feasibility plan describes the best estimate of the time it will take to get fully operational and serve a steady stream of customers or clients. This can take several years. Getting started includes gathering the needed funds, setting up whatever is needed physically to operate, hiring the key employees, developing the critical relationships and partnerships, completing the product and service design, and setting up customer or client marketing efforts. From the point of a decision to go forward after some funding has been obtained, it is often the case that this takes 6–12 months. Moving to full operations with steady customer or client interactions can take multiple years. During that time it is likely that the model will be revised based on real experience. Moving to stability and possible growth can take several more years after the model is proven sound, the revenue meets the expense needs and the outcomes are proving its success. Each venture is different with much of the variations linked to the extent of interaction time required for customers/clients and the complexity of the various products and services.

11. Measures of Progress

The final part of a venture plan is an early proposal of how the social entrepreneur will know if the plan is working. Selecting what to measure and how the relevant information will be collected is important to do at this early stage. There are three kinds of measures that should be considered. First is the measure of progress on the venture's implementation and growth. This is often called process evaluation. The budgets and timelines created in the venture feasibility plan do set the basics for this assessment and quarterly reviews of those are common ways to measure this. It is also at these review points that changes in plans, budgets, and other parts of the venture plans can be done.

The second kind of measure of progress is called outputs. These define the immediate changes or observable actions that should be seen in the target populations as they are engaged with the venture and shortly thereafter. These are the direct results of the venture's activities: numbers of meals provided, numbers of youth attending on average, numbers of products delivered, etc.[19] Outputs should not be confused with outcomes as they do not necessarily demonstrate a full change in behavior or system. But outputs are often indicators that the desired change is likely. For example, an output for a stop smoking service would be that the average client is trying at least 3 of the tools provided.

The final category of measurement is focused on assessing whether the outcomes are achieved. This requires defining how the changes in the behaviors, practices, attitudes, skills or knowledge of clients or customers will be determined. The desired outcomes of a stop smoking program are to have those served stop smoking in the short term and never smoke again in the long term. Gathering regular feedback from customers/clients will be critical to successfully measuring this. Choosing a measure at this stage allows the program services model to include what measurement efforts area needed in the service delivery plan. For example, the smoking cessation program may decide that all served will be contacted every 6 months and asked 3 questions and that a first day interview is needed.

Example of outcome measurements

- **Twin Cities RISE!—long-term outcome measure: Long-term job retention:** TCR! graduates succeed in the workplace. Among them, 81% remain in their job in the first year, and 70% remain in the second year.
- **Neighborhood Development Center: Neighborhoods focused on by NDC will see economic returns to the region and to the neighborhood economies. In 2011** our entrepreneurs returned $68 million each year to the Twin Cities regional economy, and $36 million of that is returned to inner-city neighborhood economies.

The social entrepreneur should be cautious about selecting what to measure. *"Not everything that counts can be counted and not everything that can be counted counts."* ~William Bruce Cameron (often falsely attributed to Albert Einstein).[20] At this stage the listing should describe what change looks like without worry about whether fully viable measures are available.

Summary

This chapter lays out the key elements of a social venture feasibility plan. The resulting narrative becomes a blueprint draft that then can guide the more intensive work needed to be ready to a launch. While these plans become written documents, the social entrepreneur should expect that they will evolve over time. Furthermore, sometimes a section cannot be fully completed, as there are still important, unanswered questions. Those questions are also written down and become part of the next steps needed to move to a fully complete venture plan. Once the feasibility plan is complete, then the viability of the venture can be assessed for determining the next steps. Chapter 7 describes that final part of process.

CHAPTER 7

Completing a Viability Assessment of the Venture

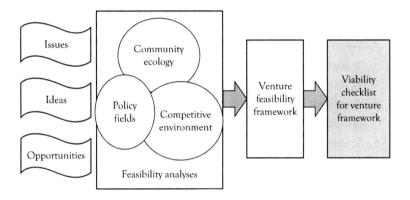

> *"Life can be understood backwards but it must be lived forwards."*
>
> Soren Kierkegaard

Learning Goals

1. Able to complete a critical review of a venture feasibility plan
2. Able to complete a logic model

At this point in venture creation it is time to pause and reflect. It is time to ask, is the venture concept really viable? Should the founding social entrepreneur move ahead with it? Two tools are introduced here to help the social entrepreneur do this and allows him to easily seek the advice of others on the "go/no-go" decision.

A Quick Check

The first step is to sit back, read the full plan, and ask if all the important key pieces are in place. Figure 7.1 is a guide for this first look. There are five aspects to pay attention to during that reading. If everything is in place, then the plan is closer to viability.

1. Vision: Is the vision of success easily understood and likely to be seen by others as possible?
2. Skills: Does it appear that the necessary skills to implement the plan are in place?
3. Incentives: Is the set of products and services likely to be embraced by the customers or clients? Is the reward for use evident and likely to be seen as positive by those intended to use the services or product?
4. Resources: Is there evidence that the needed resources will be available?
5. Action Plan: Do the actions described hang together? Is the action plan clear to a new reader?

Vision	Skills	Incentives	Resources	Action plan	Result
X	X	X	X	X	Change
No	X	X	X	X	Confusion
X	No	X	X	X	Anxiety
X	X	No	X	X	Slow change
X	X	X	No	X	Extreme frustration
X	X	X	X	No	Flase starts

Figure 7.1. Change model: diagnostic.
Source: Manning and Curtis (2008); Renaldo (2010).

Logic Model Creation

The second step is the creation of a logic model. The social venture feasibility plan guided by Chapter 6 can be tens of pages long and it is important for the founders, staff, partners, funders and more. However, logic model format provides an easier way to communicate the social entrepreneur's dreams and the basics of her thinking. She can also use the logic model as another way to determine the viability of the venture.

The *logic model* is a more visual reflection of the overall plan. Sometimes it is helpful to create this logic model first as a blue print for the full written venture feasibility plan. But most often it is easiest to complete the model after a venture feasibility plan is written. W. K. Kellogg Foundation promotes the use of the logic model because they see it as "a systematic and visual way to present and share your understanding of the relationship among the resources you need to operate your venture, the activities you plan and the changes or results you hope to achieve."[1]

The logic model is sometimes called the program outcome framework. Its origins date back to the 1970s when it was developed by evaluators Suchman and Weiss and promoted by Extension services across the country. The extension services of the University of Wisconsin continue this tradition with a website full of information about the logic model as well as tools to use in completing one. In the 1990s, the United Way of America began to promote a version of a logic model across the country as a tool to guide the development of outcome measures and as a means to gather information from the programs funded by local United Ways. W.K. Kellogg Foundation embraced it about that time as well and promoted as a tool for foundations.[2]

There are a variety of versions of a logic model, but the basic elements are consistent, as shown in figure 7.2. Its core principle is that a program, venture, or product for social purposes is best when there is a clear set of desired outcomes and where there are viable, logical links among the key elements. By visually laying out the key elements on one page, it is easier to see the logic links and to assess the areas needing further attention. The logic model format presented here is a slight variation of the one used by the United Way of America.

Assumptions	Resources	Activities	Outputs	Outcomes: Short & long term
Factors contributing to design choices	Funding, staffing, equipment, facilities	Key actions, program elements	Immediate changes	Desired results

Figure 7.2. Logic model framework.

There are five components of this logic model: Outcomes, Outputs, Activities, Resources, and Assumptions.

For what follows, we assume that the reader has completed all of the work called for in Chapter 6. In creating a logic model it is best to start at the far right of the diagram; that is, to start with the desired end in mind.

Outcomes: The first step is to write in the long-term outcomes that already have been determined. These outcomes may take up to 10 years to achieve and often occur after the connection with the people served has been completed.

Next is to enter in the shorter term outcomes—These are outcomes that will, if accomplished in a shorter period of time, likely soon after completing the service or using the product.

Outputs: Then it is time to include the Outputs. This section of the Logic Model should include the most critical immediate changes seen in the clients or customers. These were described in the measurement section of the venture feasibility plan.

Activities: Listing actions is next. Here is a list of the key activities that will be done. Using just a few words, these are shorthand descriptors of the strategies and actions chosen to engage with those to be served. These are the processes, events, products, and actions that are core to the venture.

Resources or inputs: This part of the model is a list of the most important resources that are necessary to complete the actions successfully. Included here are the human, financial, organizational, partnerships, and community resources key to delivering the venture.

Assumptions: Here the entrepreneur lists the most critical assumptions made that reinforce the logic of each of the diagram elements. As discussed in more detail in Chapter 6, it is particularly important to list the assumptions behind the selection of specific actions to be taken. The choice of actions, services, and products is usually based on a combination of research and assumptions determined from analysis of the situation and the needs of the targeted population. These assumptions should be stated as part of the logic model. Even if research is the basis for the selection, there are assumptions made about the application of that research to the specific population and community in focus. Assumptions describe the reason for the selection of the specific actions and why the short-term outcomes are expected to lead to the long-term outcomes.

Once a logic model is completed it should be reviewed by all engaged. It should be assessed to determine if the "logic" behind the venture model is sound and that links or connections between each component are reasonable.

A strong logic model will have clear and justified connections between each element. There should be an "if-then" connection between each of the key elements of a logic model.

1. If the resources necessary are available then the activities can be accomplished.
2. If the activities are accomplished then the outputs intended will hopefully be evident.
3. If the activities are accomplished and the outputs are evident, then the participants or customers will benefit as described in the short-term outcomes.
4. And if the short-term outcomes, the benefits to those reached, are achieved then the long-term outcomes might be more likely to occur.

A logic model can be used throughout the life of a venture. It can be used first to engage donors or investors. It can be used to orient new employees and to guide their work assignments. It can be used as a guide to create a program evaluation and it can be used for the basis of ongoing strategic planning.[3]

Viability Checking

The viability check list is the third tool that can help the social entrepreneur to pause and review the set of decisions and choices that have been made about the venture. It is at this point the social entrepreneur will likely be seeking support from others either as volunteers, partners, investors, or potential donors. They will be asking questions about the idea as well. This listing of questions should guide the private thinking of the social entrepreneur as well as the discussions among all who are or will be engaged or connected to the venture development. This checklist was influenced by the judging criteria used by Ideas Showcase Network managed by the University of Kentucky.[4]

1. The issue and the idea:
   a. Does the discussion of the issue detail the size and scope of the issue and the ramifications if not addressed?
   b. Are there areas that need further exploration to find more facts about the target population? Are these listed with a plan of action to gain the needed facts?
   c. Does the social entrepreneur demonstrate that he or she understands the related policy issues, government systems, and industry parameters?
2. Product or Service Idea
   a. Does the discussion of the idea seem to address a good part of the issue of concern?
   b. Is the venture product or service fully described and understandable to people not close to the venture?
   c. Is it clear how the venture will change the way people live or work?
3. Target Population
   a. Is the target population specific enough?
   b. To what degree is the target population experiencing the issue?
   c. Has information been collected directly from the target population about their interest in the product or service?
   d. Is venture likely to reach and engage with the target population given the plans to date?
4. Operations
   a. Is it clear how the venture will do its work?
   b. Does the planned staff team include the necessary expertise and amount of time needed to deliver the product or service?
   c. Have potential partnerships been identified that will be necessary to operate?
   d. Is it likely that the planned structure will enable the venture to attract the necessary revenues?
5. Timeline
   a. Does the timeline for start-up and beginning operations seem reasonable?
   b. Are the resources coming in a timely way to enable planned development?

6. Financial plan
   a. Is the budget well thought out?
   b. Are the identified sources of income feasible sources?
   c. If the customer is expected to pay, is there evidence that the target users/customers are willing to pay for your product/service?
7. Process and Outcome Evaluation
   a. Are there plans to collect and analyze information periodically to determine both progress on the plan and changes in those served?

Summary

This pause and review stage allows the Social Entrepreneur to engage advisors, colleagues, and others in this reflection as well. It is likely that some changes will be made in parts of the feasibility plan at this time, or the social entrepreneur may, at this point, decide that his or her venture is just not feasible in its present form. Regardless, the social entrepreneur has acquired a much deeper understanding of the issue to be addressed, ideas for solving the issue, and some visions of the potential for wider scale change. On the other hand, it is often the case that this review stage concludes "go forward." Then the next major effort begins—moving to deeper detailed planning and launching the venture with confidence and excitement!

Denise DeVaan: From Teacher to National Advocate Reducing Poverty

Denise DeVaan is President and CEO of DeVaan & Associates, LLC, and through a consultancy with ICF International she is currently Senior Asset Building Consultant to the Assets for Independence (AFI) Program, Federal Department of Health & Human Services, Washington, DC. In her current work she leads a team of 15 consultants working with HHS Regional staff, local grantee organizations, and partners to implement the ASSET Initiative in all 50 states. This initiative is implementing widely the lessons and practices of early demonstrations in a variety of states.

Denise began working on antipoverty public policy in the early 1980s. In 1997 Denise learned about the new field focused on financial asset building for those in poverty. She agreed that the lack of financial assets was a key factor in blocking economic progress for those living in poverty. She envisioned a program that would provide savings incentives such as a match for dollars saved combined with financial literacy education with the goal of helping people move out of poverty. Denise led the development of an early model that tested the concepts of assets for independence in Minnesota. She organized and led a 1997 state public policy campaign to win passage of the Family Assets for Independence in Minnesota (FAIM). Denise then began her consulting business to lead the design and implementation of FAIM across Minnesota. She worked through a multisite network that eventually reached nearly all 87 Minnesota counties. Network partners included community action agencies, Women Venture, various Indian Tribes, and the City County Federal Credit Union. This transformational pilot of matched savings accounts and financial education demonstrated that individuals living in poverty, when given an opportunity, could build a personal asset base, gain financial literacy, and move out of poverty.

The model builds relationships between public, nonprofit, and private organizations, especially financial institutions, at the local and state levels to combine expertise and resources to focus on ending poverty. In Minnesota low-wage workers have deposited $2 million and nationally $66 milllion in matched savings accounts. Thousands have completed financial education classes, gotten banked, purchased homes, pursued higher education, and started microenterprises. Now she is a lead consultant helping states across the United States develop their own programs.

Denise graduated from the College of Saint Benedict in 1975 with a major in Theology and later obtained a Masters in Human Development from St. Mary's University. Her service learning experiences in college set her on this path of service to others. She first was an elementary school teacher. She soon realized that she needed to do more when she observed that her students came to school hungry. She left teaching to focus on social policies and programs to reduce poverty working for the Catholic Charities of Minneapolis. Mid-career she was selected to receive the prestigious National Kellogg Fellows Leadership Award that allowed her interaction with the leaders of the most dynamic social change efforts in the world. Her Kellogg leadership studies in Northern Ireland, South Africa, Cost Rica, Brazil, Mexico, and the United States provided a new understanding of how to build cross-sector partnerships to change how people living in poverty are assisted and to building dynamic coalitions that get results. Denise is active in volunteer leadership roles in national organizations focused on ending poverty

APPENDIX II

Frey Foundation (Minnesota): A Story of a Journey from Charity to Systems Change Engagement by Terri Barreiro

The Frey Foundation was formed in 1997 after the sale of a family-owned company. This small family foundation engages three generations in its philanthropic decisions. Jim Frey is the part-time staff person and also a member of the Board of Trustees. On June 25, 2010 Jim told the story of the foundation's systems change engagement to Terri Barreiro, Executive-in-Residence and member of the Philanthropy and Public Policy Initiative team at the Humphrey Institute's Center for Public and Nonprofit Leadership.

> *The mission of Frey Foundation and its affiliate philanthropies is to be a catalyst in strengthening its community through effective, direct giving which promotes self sufficiency and stimulates creative change, resulting in improved quality of life for all.*

In the Beginning Years

The Frey Foundation Board of Trustees guides funding from the foundation assets and donor-advised funds housed at Catholic Community Foundation and The St. Paul Foundation (TSPF). The family has a long history with the TSPF and when the foundation was first forming advisors from that community foundation provided advice and expertise to help them get started.

In the beginning years, the mission of the foundation was broadly stated. Grants were made responding to requests and following family member interests. There were no site visits and the family-only board met 1–2 times a year to make decisions. Much of the grants were tied to the interests of the founding members. The foundation leadership was spending a lot of time during those early years developing an investment strategy for the foundation assets and completing all that was necessary for organization formation.

Getting More of a Focus

After those early years the second generation, Jim Frey and his sister Carol Frey Wolfe, were asked by their father to get more engaged. Jim was asked to assume the President's role and continue his board trustee role. About that same time, in 2003, the investment decision process was determined to be well established, allowing staff time to be dedicated to improving the impact of grants.

First Jim led the Foundation Trustees to take time to look back at the grants that had been made. They studied what the trends were in the grants made and set the stage for a planning retreat of the Trustees. That retreat concluded that the grants were too diffused across too many areas and that it would be better to focus on one thing. At the retreat the trustees also determined that the primary focus should be providing a decent place to live for those who were homeless or precariously housed.

Why did that focus get selected? As Jim tells the story, his mother was a volunteer with Catholic Charities while the children were growing up. When she volunteered she would often bring the children along. They visited shelters and food shelves, often becoming volunteers themselves. The children were able to get to know some of the people served by those programs and realized they were good people facing difficult life situations.

In the review of the grants history Trustees noted that grants had already been made by the foundation to a number of organizations working on homelessness issues. This gave them a base to build on for their new focus. With a new single focus it did mean others that had been funded in the past were told that no further funding would be available.

Implementing that focus took some time. Throughout the process of changing to a specific focus, Jim worked to keep the trustees informed bringing them to important meetings and bringing experts to Board meetings. He also said he developed thick skin as saying "no" to good organizations that didn't match the priority was very hard.

Finding Partners

It was fortunate that at the same time this focus was selected community leaders and the governor, Tim Pawlenty, were also engaging in more intense action to address homelessness. The governor had set a challenge, "to end homelessness by 2010." A comprehensive community plan had been completed and a state office to coordinate this action had been established with strong engagement of state offices and nonprofit leaders.

Jim Frey went to meet with the governor to see how his family's foundation could assist. He learned that government funds were focused on creating the bricks and mortar of housing but there were very limited State dollars addressing the services needs of those they expected to house in the new and rehabilitated construction.

Jim knew from experience and conversations with those the foundation was funding that the people who were homeless had challenges including chemical dependency, mental health problems, lack of high school diploma, and little or no employment experience. He knew services would be needed to transition people to stable lives after they moved into stable housing. Jim talked to family members who shared his concerns and interest in doing more to help the governor's challenge to be a success.

In 2006, the Frey Foundation stepped up with a pledge of five million dollars in funding for services to be granted over the next five years. Governor Pawlenty held a joint press conference to announce this new foundation partnership encouraging others to follow the Frey Foundation lead. The partnership agreement was that the state would continue to provide funding and leadership for construction and the Frey Foundation would support the needed services.

Jim then began discussions with other family foundations encouraging them to join in the effort. These foundations had longer traditions of grantmaking and more existing focused efforts. But after some time a number of them too joined the effort to address homelessness. This allowed significant expansion of services to match the significant expansion of housing construction that was funded with government dollars.

Strengthening the Focus

This new partnership galvanized the trustees around this focus and they dedicated themselves to better understanding of the issue and strong grantmaking to ensure their partner pledge was successfully executed.

Advice from experts was important for the Freys. The McKnight Foundation, which has been deeply engaged in affordable housing for a long time, provided advice to the Frey Foundation. Nonprofit organizations highly regarded for their affordable housing agendas became resources for the Frey Foundation including the Family Housing Fund, Corporation for Supportive Housing, Wilder Foundation, and Greater Minnesota Housing Fund.

The Frey Foundation selected grantees that had strong reputations and proven success in stabilizing the lives of clients. Fifteen organizations became primary partners with the Frey Foundation to address the homelessness issue. Jim engaged in deeper conversations with the leaders of those organizations seeking ways to leverage the foundation grants. Each grant was framed to address important priorities for that organization. Often these grants were designed to increase the amount of funds coming from individual donors as that was often a weakness Jim observed. The frequent result was significant improvement in the number of individual gifts as well as the amount of the average gift.

By the end of three years, in 2009, nearly all of the $5 million committed to the initiative had been spent or pledged. That was 1½ years ago. The board considered the situation, the need, and their progress and made the decision to commit another $5 million. With that in hand Jim Frey recruited other private foundation partners to join him in encouraging the state of Minnesota to continue its commitment to affordable housing despite a downturn in the economy.

A New Public Private Partnership Is Formed

About this same time a new collaborative was forming in Hennepin County called Heading Home Hennepin. It was organized by Hennepin County leaders and its agenda was to be much more aggressive about ending homelessness in the Minneapolis area. Jim was invited to join the discussions to help find ways to leverage the county funds. As a result of Jim and other's work, foundation, business, faith community and individual donations are now part of the funds used for Heading Home Hennepin.

Jim and others very much liked the Hennepin collaborative model. So he along with Carleen Rhodes, President of The Saint Paul Foundation and Minnesota Community Foundation, and Laura Kadwell, Minnesota's Director of Ending Long-Term Homelessness, and others helped form Heading Home Minnesota with the goal of creating homelessness focused efforts at the local level in Minnesota. Today Heading Home Minnesota is a statewide initiative to end homelessness and is the umbrella organization for 10 regional initiatives. Its business plan to end homelessness has three primary goals:

1. Create supportive housing to stop the cycle of homelessness.
2. Provide stop-gap assistance and discharge initiatives.
3. Reach out to homeless youth and adults on the streets.

Continued research about the issue, public education, local focused dialogues around what will work best and new construction tied to services are all strategies used by Head Home Minnesota (HHMn). Funding for HHMn projects now include federal dollars from HUD and Fannie Mae. As of the interview, over 4,500 new units have been constructed. Other states have sought advice from HHMn for their own ending homelessness strategies.

Trustee Engagement

Trustee education at the Frey Foundation continues to be a priority. Board meeting agendas were changed reducing the detailed discussions about specific grants by using strong write-ups and a consent agenda format. This freed up time for expanded issue education and discussion. Speakers to the Board have included leaders of government agency partners and other opinion leaders, moving the discussions to a much deeper level about the issues of concern. Trustees also go on site visits and attend major meetings on the issues. Constant communication is part of the foundations engagement success. It happens both informally during family member to family member conversations as well as formal foundation communication.

The foundation also has changed how it reviews proposals, reviewing all proposals for affordable housing at the same meeting. Another newer focus candidate for the foundation is early childhood education and it is following the same strategy that was used to focus on affordable housing.

The foundation now has detailed plans for its work in affordable housing, well-informed trustees and trust in how the staff is working on behalf of the foundation. The foundation has a much longer time horizon for this initiative and the trustees know that precludes engagement on many other topics.

Going Beyond Grantmaking

Recently the Board of Trustees approved investing some of their assets as Program Related Investments with two longtime partner nonprofit organizations. Jim continues to seek out new strategies to leverage the investment possibilities of the Frey Foundation. For example, he is currently exploring ways to assist local entrepreneurs to formalize their own community involvement by focusing attention on successful models such as Social Venture Partners Minnesota.

The Frey Foundation is now recognized as a philanthropic leader in the affordable housing issue arena. Jim Frey is co-chair of Heading Home Minnesota's Steering Committee and actively engaged in formal and informal discussions in the community about this issue. While Jim would not describe himself as a leader, as there are other much larger foundations deeply engaged, Jim says "If it were baseball I guess I would say I am on the AAA team, but not a Major League player."

Jim believes that continued questioning about what works and why along with the door- opening resource of foundation funds can do much to move the agenda forward. He says, "It is fulfilling and hard work. I am very glad we are doing it; our impact is on people whose lives are changed and who now have the tools to succeed."

Responding to a Changing Environment

Today the homelessness issue is facing new challenges. Unfortunately, due to the economy and the housing foreclosure crisis, more people are homeless today. And more of those who were living in newly built stabilized housing have lost their jobs and once again need added services to regain life stability. The Frey Foundation works closely with its partners to refine their goals and move quickly to change what is being done collectively to respond effectively to the changing environment.

Conclusion

The Frey Foundation commitment to Affordable Housing is entering its 7th year. The foundation is engaged as a grantmaker, an investor, a partner with nonprofits, a partner with other foundations, a partner with government, an educator of themselves and others and as a leader in finding the best solutions and doing the hard work it takes to implement them.

Mike Temali: Expert in Neighborhood and Economic Transformation

Mihailo (Mike) Temali is the founder and executive director of the Neighborhood Development Center (NDC) and the founder and president of Western Initiatives for Neighborhood Development (WIND), both in St. Paul, Minnesota.

Neighborhood Development Center started in St. Paul Minnesota and now serves communities across the Twin Cities. This organization identifies potential entrepreneurs who may be operating microenterprises out of their homes, have a work ethic, technical skills and entrepreneurial ideas. It then provides training, microloans and support services to help them grow. Temali's organization uses a business incubator model designed to help entrepreneurs overcome those barriers.

A reporter for Minnesota Public Radio interviewed Mike Temali in 2008. "Small businesses are key to any neighborhood revitalization effort. If it's all run down and half empty, they write off the neighborhood but if it seems to be thriving they think 'Maybe I can shop here, maybe I can start a business here or buy a house, move here, whatever," said Temali. "So, the commercial corridor (in a neighborhood) and its stock of small businesses and small buildings is pretty key as not only an indicator but as a catalyst, a tool for changing what happens in the future."[1]

The impact of Neighborhood Development Center can be seen in the thriving Midtown Global Market on Lake Street in Minneapolis and in the Plaza Latina mini-mall on St. Paul's Payne Avenue. Each location provides small retail spaces, peer support, expert coaching and financial assistance for entrepreneur tenants. Sharing space means cheaper rent, more customers and visibility.

Working in five languages, English, Hmong, Oromo, Somali, and Spanish and in 12 low-income neighborhoods, the NDC staff has trained over 3,800 entrepreneurs in a 16-week class, and assisted more than 600 people with entrepreneurial talent in starting their own businesses. The NDC has also developed the first loan program acceptable to the Islamic community, opening new opportunities to Muslim entrepreneurs.

Previously, Temali was executive director of North End Area Revitalization, Inc. (NEAR), also in St. Paul. Temali earned a master's degree in public affairs at the University of Minnesota's Humphrey Institute. As a Bush Leadership Fellow in 1998, he studied at Harvard and MIT, and did development work in Santiago, Chile. In 2007 he presented the NDC's model to the trustees of the Ford Foundation. Temali has written a signature book on development, *The Community Economic Development Handbook*, used by community developers everywhere

Temali grew up on St. Paul's East Side, the son of World War II refugees, who devoted their lives to improving the lives of others.

Notes

Chapter 1

1. Retrieved from http://minnesota.publicradio.org/display/web/2008/02/10 /immigrantbusiness
2. Wilder Foundation (n.d.) *Statewide Homeless Study Results* Retrieved from http://www.wilder.org/Wilder-Research/Research-Areas/Homelenessess /Pages/default.aspx
3. The Water Project. (n.d) . *Why Water* Retrieved from http://thewaterproject. org/why-water.php
4. Polio Global Eradication Initiative (n.d.) *Infected Countries.* Retrieved from http://www.polioeradication.org/Infectedcountries.aspx
5. Alvord, Brown, and Letts (2004).
6. Dees (1998); Light (2009); Martin and Osberg (2007).
7. Stone (2002).
8. Private Interview by Terri Barreiro with Tim Reardon, Minneapolis-based consultant and initiative leader for social issue collaborations, completed February 17, 2013.
9. Rothschild (2012), p. xi.
10. Friedman and McGarvie (2008), p. 38.
11. Friedman and McGarvie (2008), p. 227.
12. Douglas (1987).
13. Frumkin (2002).
14. Clemens (2006).
15. Skloot (1987).
16. Jenkins (2006).
17. Brown (1998).
18. Anheier and Salamon (2006).
19. Billis (2010); Smith (2010).
20. Ebrahim (2012).
21. Family Asset Independence in Minnesota. (2011). *Homepage.* Retrieved from http://minnesotafaim.com/index.cfm
22. Children's Defense Fund. (2012). *About Us.* Retrieved from http://www .childrensdefense.org/about-us/
23. Minnesota Public Radio (2013). *About Us.* Retrieved from http://minnesota. publicradio.org/about/mpr/.

24. Students Today Leaders Forever (2013), *Homepage.* Retrieved from http://www.stlf.net/home

25. Teach for America. (n.d.) *Our History.* Retrieved from http://www.teachforamerica.org/our-organization/our-history

26. Twin Cities Rise (2012) *What we Accomplish.* Retrieved from http://twincitiesrise.org/about-us/what-we-accomplish.html

27. Grameen Bank. (2013) *A Short History.* Retrieved from http://www.grameen-info.org/index.php?option=com_content&task=view&id=19&Itemid=114

28. Neighborhood Development Center, (2013). Retreived from *About. http://www.ndc-mn.org/about*

29. Acumen Fund. (2013) *Homepage.* Retrieved from http://acumen.org/ten/

Chapter 2

1. Brooks (2009), p. 7.
2. Guclu, Dees, and Anderson (2002).
3. Tim Reardon, 3–1–03 interview with Terri Barreiro.
4. Kingdon (1995).
5. Skoll (2010).
6. Ashoka Innovators for the Public. (2013). *What is a Social Entrepreneurship?* Retrieved from https://www.ashoka.org/social_entrepreneur
7. Swallow (2012).
8. Drucker (1985).
9. Drucker (1985).
10. Herbert (2011).
11. Denise DeVaan interview 6–25–11.

Chapter 3

1. Brooks (2009), p. 24.
2. Brooks (2009), p. 177.
3. Kickul and Lyons (2012), p. 55.
4. Brooks (2009), pp. 23–31.
5. Wheelen and Hunger (2006).
6. Levine, Perkins, and Perkins (2005).
7. The Community Ecosystems Circles Model builds on concepts first written about by Urie Bronfenbrenner, when he described the interaction of children within their family and their family within their routine environment. It was originally published by Urie Bronfenbrenner (1979) in *The Ecology of Human*

Development. Marilyn Larson adapted that first model as she provided staff leadership for the Minnesota Action for Children Commission in the early 1990s. Barreiro was a member of the Commission and participated in the model development discussions. The resulting model added the human dynamics for a child of the interactions of family and their surrounding environment. Using the expanded model the Action for Children Commission incorporated roles of government policies and of public attitudes in this ever more complex social ecology framework. That model for planning was then used by Barreiro in United Way community planning discussions. Those dialogues expanded the model with one more component of the concentric circles to acknowledge the role that professional interventive institutions do play.

8. Bronfenbrenner (1979), pp. 3–9.
9. Cooperrider, Whitney and Stavros (2008).
10. Bronfenbrenner (1979), p. 8.

Chapter 4

1. Rothschild (2012), p. 23.
2. Sandfort and Stone (2008).
3. Adapted from Sandfort (2010).
4. Adapted from Sandfort (2010).
5. DiMaggio (1988); Fligstein (2001).
6. Kingdon (1995); Stone (2002).
7. Stone and Sandfort (2009).
8. Burstein (1991); Laumann and Knoke (1987).
9. Salamon (2002).
10. Bryson, Cunningham, and Lokkesmoe (2004).
11. Sandfort (2010).
12. Provan et al. (2005).

Chapter 5

1. Porter (1980).
2. Lindenberg (2001).
3. Brooks (2009).
4. Rothschild (2012).
5. Oster (1995).
6. Oster (1995).

7. Note that Oster (1995) separates "buyers" into two categories—the users or beneficiaries of the service or program and donors. She does not include donors as "suppliers" but rather emphasizes in this category labor suppliers. We prefer the categorization we use in this chapter because it emphasizes a broader view of "suppliers" to include several types of resources.
8. Rothschild (2012).
9. Smith and Lipsky (1993).

Chapter 6

1. McNamara Carter. (n.d.). *The basics of developing mission, vision, and values statements.* Retrieved from http://managementhelp.org/strategicplanning/misson-vision-values.htm
2. Foundation Center. (n.d.). *Establishing a Nonprofit Organization.* Retrieved from www.foundationcenter.org/getstarted/tutorials/establish/statements.html
3. Teach For America. (n.d.). Retrieved from www.teachforamerica.org/our-mission
4. Good Will Industries International, Inc. (2009, September 8). Retrieved from www.goodwill.org/about-us/goodwills-heritage-mission-vision-and-values
5. www.nature.org/about-us/vision-mission/index.htm
6. Twin Cities Rise!. Fact Sheet (n.d.) retrieved from http://twincitiesrise.org/documents
7. Kanter (2012).
8. Snicket (2009).
9. Anderson (2005).
10. Teach for America. (n.d.). Retrieved from http://www.teachforamerica.org/why-teach-for-america/building-a-movement
11. DeVaan, Denise. (interview with Terri Barreiro, August 2012)
12. Shapiro, Marla (2012, June 13). Retrieved from http://www.ctvnews.ca/health/healthblog/dr-marla-shapiro-simple-changes-can-cause-domino-effect-weight-loss-1.823232
13. The Roberts Enterprise Development Fund (REDF) (2005, December) *If the Shoe Fits: Nonprofit or For-Profit: The Choice Matters.* Dec 2005 Retrieved form http://www.redf.org/learn-from-redf/publications/123
14. Collins Dictionary. (n.d.). Retrieved from http://www.collinsdictionary.com/dictionary/english
15. United Way of America. (1996). UW Measuring Program Outcomes: A Practical Approach. pg. xv. Retrieved from http://www.unitedwaycv.org/media/Measuring_Program_Outcomes-UW.pdf

16. W. K. Kellogg Foundation. (2004). *Logic Model Development Guide.* Retrieved from http://www.wkkf.org/knowledge-center/resources/2006 /02/WK-Kellogg-Foundation-Logic-Model-Development-Guide.aspx

17. University of Wisconsin Extension Services (2003, February). *Enhancing Program Performance With Logic Models Online course.* Retrived at http:// www.uwex.edu/ces/lmcourse/ pg 85

18. Urban Institute. (n.d.) *Outcomes Indicators Project.* Retrieved from http:// www.urban.org/center/cnp/Projects/outcomeindicators.cfm

19. United Way of America. (1996). *UW Measuring Program Outcomes: A Practical Approach.* pg. xv. (Retrieved from http://www.unitedwaycv.org /media/Measuring_Program_Outcomes-UW.pdf

20. Quote Investigator Retrieved at http://quoteinvestigator.com/tag/william-bruce-cameron/

Chapter 7

1. W. K. Kellogg Logic Model Development Guide (2004), pp. 1–13.
2. Henert and Taylor-Powell (2008).
3. W. K. Kellogg Logic Model Development Guide (2004), p. 22.
4. University of Kentucky Appalachian Center—Ideas Showcase Network

Appendix III

1. Retrieved from http://minnesota.publicradio.org/display/web/2008/02/10/ immigrantbusiness

References

Alvord, S. H., Brown, L. D., & Letts, C. W. (2004). Social entrepreneurship and societal transformation: An exploratory study. *Journal of Applied Behavioral Science, 40*(3), 260–282.

Anderson, A. A. (2005). *The community builder's approach to theory of change: A practical guide to theory development.* Washington D.C.: The Aspen Institute.

Anheier, H. K., & Salamon, L. (2006). The nonprofit sector in comparative perspective. *The nonprofit sector: A research handbook,* (2nd ed), (pp. 89–114). New Haven, CT: Yale University Press.

Billis, D. (2010). From welfare bureaucracies to welfare hybrids. In D. Billis (ed.), *Hybrid organizations and the third sector.* London: Palgrave Macmillan.

Bronfenbrenner, U. (1979). *The ecology of human development.* Cambridge, MA: Harvard University Press.

Brooks, A. C. (2009). *Social entrepreneurship: A modern approach to social value creation.* Saddle River, NJ: Pearson Education, Inc.

Brown, L. D. (1998). Creating social capital: nongovernmental development organizations and intersectoral problem solving. In W. W. Powell and E. S. Clemens (eds.), *Private action for the public good,* (pp. 283–287). New Haven, CT: Yale University Press.

Bryson, J. M., Cunningham, G. L., & Lokkesmoe, K. J. (2004). What to do when stakeholders matter: The case of problem formulation for the African American men project of Hennepin County, Minnesota. *Public Administration Review, 62*(5), 568–584.

Burstein, P. (1991). Policy domains: organization, culture, and policy outcomes. *Annual Review of Sociology, 17,* 327–350.

Cameron, W. B. (1963). *Informal sociology: A casual introduction to sociological thinking.* New York: Random House.

Clemens, E. (2006). The constitution of citizens: Political theories of nonprofit organizations. In W. W. Powell & R. Steinberg (eds.), *The nonprofit sector: A research handbook,* (2nd ed), (pp. 207–220). New Haven, CT: Yale University Press.

Cooperrider, D. L., Whitney, D, & Stavros, J. M. (2008). *Appreciative inquiry handbook* (2nd ed.). Brunswick, OH: Crown Custom Publishing, Inc.

Dees, J. G. (1998). *The meaning of social entrepreneurship.* Self-published essay. Revised May 2001. Available at www.caseatduke.org/documents/dees_sedef.pdf.

DiMaggio, P. J. (1988). Interest and agency in institutional theory. In L. Zucker (ed.), *Institutional patterns and organizations: Culture and environment* (pp. 3–22). Cambridge, MA: Ballinger Publishing Company.

Douglas, J. (1987). Political theories of nonprofit organizations. In W. W. Powell (ed.), *The nonprofit sector: A research handbook* (pp. 43–54). New Haven, CT: Yale University Press.

Drucker, P. (1985). *Innovation and entrepreneurship*. New York: HarperCollins Publishing.

Ebrahim, A. (2012). Enacting our field. Keynote address. *Nonprofit Management & Leadership, 23*(1), 13–28.

Fligstein, N. (2001). Social skill and the theory of fields. *Sociological Theory, 19*(2), 105–125.

Friedman, L. J., & McGarvie, M. D. (2008). *Charity, philanthropy, and civility in American history*. NY: Cambridge University Press.

Frumkin, P. (2002). *On being nonprofit*. Cambridge, MA: Harvard University Press.

Guclu, A., Dees, G., & Anderson, B. B. (2002). *The process of social entrepreneurship: Creating opportunities worthy of serious pursuit*. Durham, NC: Center for the Advancement of Social Entrepreneurship, Duke University.

Henert, E., & Taylor-Powell, E. (2008). *Developing a logic model: Teaching and training guide. Madison, WI:* University of Wisconsin-Extension, Program Development and Evaluation. http://www.uwex.edu/ces/pdande/evaluation/pdf/lmguidecomplete.pdf

Herbert, M. (November, 1, 2010). *The iPad—breaking new ground in special education* district adminstration magazine. Retrieved from: http://www.districtadministration.com/article/ipad%E2%80%94breaking-new-ground-special-education

Jenkins, J. C. (2006). Nonprofit organizations and political advocacy. *The nonprofit sector: A research handbook,* (2nd ed). New Haven, CT: Yale University Press, pp. 307–332.

Kanter, R. M. (September 25, 2012). *Ten reasons people resist change. HBR Blog Network*. Retrieved from http://blogs.hbr.org/kanter/2012/09/ten-reasons-people-resist-chang.html

Kickul, J., & Lyons, T. (2012). *Understanding social entrepreneurship: The relentless pursuit of mission in an ever changing world*. New York, NY: Routledge.

Kingdon, J. W. (1995). *Agendas, alternatives, and public policies*. New York: Longman.

Laumann, E. O., & Knoke, D. (1987). *The organization state: Social choice in national policy domains*. Madison, WI: The University of Wisconsin Press.

Levine, M., Perkins, D. D., & Perkins, D. V. (2005). *Principles of community psychology*. New York, NY: Oxford University Press.

Light, P. (2008). *The search for social entrepreneurship.* Washington, DC: Brookings Institution Press.

Lindenberg, M. (2001). Are we at the cutting edge or the blunt edge? *Nonprofit Management and Leadership, 11*(3), 247–270.

Manning, G., & Curtis, K. (2008). *The art of leadership.* London: McGraw-Hill.

Martin, R. L., & Osberg, S. (2007). *Social entrepreneurship: The case for definition. Stanford Social Innovation Review.* (2013) Retrieved from *http://www.ssireview.org/articles/entry/social_entrepreneurship_the_case_for_definition*

Oster, S. (1995). *Strategic management for nonprofit organizations.* NY: Oxford University Press.

Porter, M. (1980). *Competitive strategy.* Old Tappen, NJ: Macmillan.

Provan, K. G., Veazie, M. A., Staten, L. K., & Teufel-Shone, N. I. (2005). The use of network analysis to strengthen community partnerships. *Public Administration Review, 65*(5), 603–613.

Renaldo, C. (October 8, 2010). *The Diagram for organisational success (and confusion, anxiety, gradual change, frustration, and false starts). sideways thoughts.* Retrieved June 27, 2013 from http://www.sidewaysthoughts.com/blog/?s=organisational+success+and+confusion

Rothschild, S. (2012). *The non nonprofit: For-profit thinking for nonprofit success.* San Fransisco CA: Jossey-Bass Publisher.

Salamon, L. M. (ed). (2002). *The state of nonprofit America: For-profit thinking for nonprofit success.* Washington, D.C.: Brookings Institution Press.

Sandfort, J., & Stone, M. M. (2008). Analyzing policy fields: Helping students understand complex state and local contexts. *Journal of Public Affairs Education, 14*(2), 129–148.

Sandfort, Jodi. (2010). Nonprofits within policy fields. *Journal of Policy Analysis and Management, 29*(3), 637–644.

Skloot, E. (1987). Enterprise and commerce in nonprofit organizations. In W.W. Powell (ed.), *The Nonprofit sector: A research handbook.* New Haven, CT: Yale University Press, pp. 380–393.

Skoll, J. (2011). *Opening remarks at 2010 Skoll World Forum: "From Curiosity to a Force in Society."* Retrieved from http://www.skollfoundation.org/jeff-skoll-opening-remarks-at-2010-skoll-world-forum-from-curiosity-to-a-force-in-society/

Smith, S. R. (2010). Hybridization and nonprofit organizations: The governance challenge. *Policy and Society, 29*(3), 219–229.

Smith, S. R., & Lipsky, M. (1993). *Nonprofits for hire.* Cambridge, MA: Harvard University Press.

Snicket, L. (2009). *A series of unfortunate events #5: The Austere academy.* Harper Collins

Stone, D. (2002). *Policy paradox, Revised edition.* New York: W.W. Norton & Company.

Stone, M. M., Sandfort, M. (2009). Building a policy fields framework to inform research on nonprofit organizations. *Nonprofit and Voluntary Sector Quarterly, 38*(6), 1054–1075.

Swallow, E. (April 19, 2012). *Can* innovative thinking be learned? *Forbes.* Retrieved June 27, 2013 from http://www.forbes.com/sites/ericaswallow/2012/04/19/innovators-dna-hal-gregersen-interview/

W. K. Kellogg Foundation. (2004) W. K. Kellogg logic model development guide, Retrieved from http://www.wkkf.org/knowledge-center/resources/2006/02/wk-kellogg-foundation-logic-model-development-guide.aspx

Wheelen, T. L., & Hunger, J. D. (2006). *Strategic management and business policy.* Upper Saddle River, NJ: Prentice Hall.

Index

CPSIA information can be obtained at www.ICGtesting.com
Printed in the USA
LVOW10s1430101213

364705LV00011B/146/P